Inventory of 15th Century Bassedanze, Balli & Balletti

in italian dance manuals

by W. Thomas Marrocco

Cord 1981
Dance Research Annual XIII

CORD Inc. Dance Research Annual XIII

Address all correspondence to: CORD Editorial Board, Editorial and Subscription Office, NYU Dance and Dance Educ. Dept., 35 West Fourth Street, Rm. 675, New York, N.Y. 10003.

LIBRARY OF CONGRESS CATALOGUE NUMBER 81-67677.

Printed in the United States of America: Spett Printing Company, Inc.

New York: Congress on Research in Dance, Inc.

In memory of my wife,
Audrey
1913–1979

and my daughter,
Sandra Beth
1946–1980

Foreword

Interest in reconstructing dances from the past has grown at a feverish pace during the past ten years or more as the study of dance history takes its legitimate place among academic and aesthetic disciplines of the field. No longer satisfied with vague generalities or impressionistic interpretations, the dancer of today claims the right to see and experience dance heritage in much the same way musicians and painters have shared their own heritage for years. Groups devoted to the authentication of period dance works are springing up across America and Europe; their research, interpretation and performances provide insight into the past, understanding for the future.

To this end, the Inventory endeavors to serve us. W. Thomas Marrocco, distinguished musicologist, has turned his love for Italian dances of the *quattrocento* into a compilation of annotated sources replete with useful content for dance scholars. Northern Italy in the dawn of the Renaissance provides the earliest dance manuals extant in the Western European cultural tradition. Because so few of the dances have been translated, scholars depend on original sources for materials—now made infinitely easier to locate and compare through use of the Inventory. Secondary materials are also listed, supplying supportive information. Finally, Dr. Marrocco's interpretation of the music notation according to current musicological practice renders the music of the dances accessible and possibly closer to performance practice of the fifteenth century.

This volume is a welcome addition to dance scholarship. It is our hope that it will inspire further interpretations of theories and choreographies contained in the manuscripts examined.

Emma Lewis Thomas

Acknowledgements

I am indebted to Dr. Emma Lewis Thomas, professor of dance, University of California, Los Angeles, for the many hours spent together wedding the choreographies to their music and tempi with dance speeds, and whose valued counsel I gratefully heeded; to Dr. Ingrid Brainard, distinguished musicologist and director of the Cambridge Court Dancers for her numerous suggestions during the final stages of this work; to Dr. Patricia A. Rowe, professor and chairman, Department of Dance and Dance Education, New York University, and Dianne L. Woodruff, Faculty of Fine Arts/Dance, York University, Canada, both of whom had understood the need for the Inventory some time ago; and, of course, my thanks to those generous librarians at the Bibliothèque Nationale, Paris; the Biblioteca Nazionale Centrale and the Biblioteca Medicea-Laurenziana, Florence; the Biblioteca Apostolica Vaticana, Rome; the Biblioteca Estense, Modena; the Biblioteca Comunale degli Intronati, Siena; the Biblioteca L. Jacobilli of the Seminario Vescovile, Foligno; and the New York Public Library, without whose kindnesses in making their precious manuscripts available to me, this work would have remained a delightful though fruitless fantasy. Finally, my gratitude to the University of California, Los Angeles, for a grant which enabled me to examine the manuscripts at first hand.

W. Thomas Marrocco

Preface

A thorough study of fifteenth century Italian dances can be achieved only when the entire corpus of choreographies and music is made available. Here, then, is the first step toward that goal—an inventory designed to guide all those interested in the theory and performance of courtly dances and the role these played in the social mores of renaissance Italy.*

Dancing was indeed considered essential to the education of a *gentildonna* and *gentiluomo* in the fifteenth century, but even a century earlier we have evidence from the pen of Giovanni Boccaccio, who informs us in his *Decamerone* that, as part of the diurnal entertainment, the women and men indulged in *balli*, *danze* and *carole*. There are reports of other auspicious occasions such as the reception accorded Pope Calixtus III and Duke Adolphe of Clèves upon their arrival in Milan 26 February 1450, where their host, Francesco Sforza, participated in courtly dances; and the presence of the pontiff, Pius II, in Florence during the last days of April and the first days of May 1459, when prominent Florentines performed *bassedanze* and *balli* in the *piazza Santa Croce*.

Giovanni Ambrogio (né Guglielmo Ebreo da Pesaro), present at many banquets and *balli* in Italian courts, has left us a refreshing account of the major role given to courtly dances in his descriptions of personages in attendance, their extravagant costumes, delectable cuisine and the *balli* and *moresche* of which he, as dance master, had the sole responsibility. (See *PBN 476,* ff. 72r–80r.)

It was Domenico da Piacenza, however, who first recognized the need to record the repertory of dances. Some of these choreographies (including French *bassedanses*) are currently being reconstructed by such dance historians as Ingrid Brainard, Angene Feves, Wendy Hilton, Bahla Jones, Julia Sutton, Emma Lewis Thomas, Shirley Wynne and others both here and in Europe. A number of these dances—Labanotated with every movement graphically prescribed—are on file with the Dance Notation Bureau, New York City. All such records are indispensable to dancers interested in recreating dances of the past with the accuracy available through research endeavors today.

---

*Ingrid Brainard's contribution to our knowledge of Renaissance dances is enormous. Her impressive doctoral dissertation, *Die Choreographie der Hoftänze in Burgund, Frankreich und Italien im 15. Jahrhundert*, Göttingen, 1956, should be examined by all dance scholars. Available now on microfilm only, it is hoped that it will make its appearance in the English language in the not too distant future.

Contents

El bel danzar che con virtù s' acquista
Per dar piacer all' anima gentile
Conforta il cuor & fa' l più signorile
& porge con dolceza allegra vista.

GUGLIELMO EBREO DA PESARO
Pratica seu arte tripudii
vulgare opusculum, 1463.

Section A

Inventory of the Choreographies

a list of the dances and their sources

Editorial Commentary: Dances

The manuscripts are listed in an approximate chronological order. Among the Guglielmo manuals I have selected *PBN 973* as the earliest and, therefore, the closest to the original. All other manuals by this dancing master have been collated with *PBN 973*. Choreographies bearing the same title in later manuscripts have been collated to detect differences in steps and movements. When two or more choreographies differ but share the same title, I have listed them separately. The number of dancers is usually given with the title, but in those instances where number and gender is not specified, the information was usually gleaned from the choreography. If lacking there, I have assumed that all participants perform as one body. *NYPL* (with *FML*) is the latest of Guglielmo's versions, undoubtedly written towards the end of his career, since there are thirteen added dances not found in his earlier manuscripts. Inasmuch as Guglielmo adopted the name Giovanni Ambrogio after his conversion to Catholicism, I have arbitrarily chosen to add both names, i.e., Guglielmo/Giovanni to those choreographies in *NYPL* without ascriptions.

I. Abbreviations, Sigla and Bibliography

ABBREVIATIONS AND SIGLA

Library			Manuscript
1.	**PBN**	= Paris, Bibliothèque Nationale	*fonds it. 972*
2.	**FBJ**	= Foligno, Biblioteca Jacobilli	*D.I. 42*
3.	**PBN**	= Paris, Biblothèque Nationale	*fonds it. 973*
4.	**RBV**	= Rome, Biblioteca Apostolica Vaticana	*Capponiano 203*
5.	**FBNC**	= Florence, Biblioteca Nazionale Centrale	*Magliabecchiana–Strozziana, XIX. 88*
6.	**SBC**	= Siena, Biblioteca Comunale	*L. V. 29*
7.	**MBE**	= Modena, Biblioteca Estense (Olim Palatina)	*Ital. 82, a.J.9.4.* (Olim VII. A. 82)
8.	**PBN**	= Paris, Bibliothèque Nationale	*fonds it. 476*
9.	**FML**	= Florence, Biblioteca Medicea–Laurenziana	*Antinori 13*
10.	**NYPL**	= New York Public Library, Dance Collection, Lincoln Center	*MGZMBZ–Res. 72–254*

BIBLIOGRAPHY

Apel, Willi. "A Remark about the Basse Danse," *Journal of Renaissance and Baroque Music*, I (1946), 139–143.

Apel, Willi. *History of Keyboard Music to 1700.* Bloomington, University of Indiana Press, 1972.

Becherini, Bianca. "L'Arte della danza di Guglielmo da Pesaro," *La Scala*, No. 84 (1956), 20–24.

BianchiT   = Bianchi, Dante. "Un trattato inedito di Domenico da Piacenza," *La Bibliofilia*, LXV (1963) 109–149.

BianchiMD   = Bianchi, Dante. "Tre maestri di danza alla corte Sforzesca," *Archivo Storico Lombardo*, LXXXIX (1962), 290–299.

BrainBBB   = Brainard, Ingrid. "Bassedanse, Bassadanza and Ballo in the 15th Century," in *Dance History Research: Perspectives from Related Arts and Disciplines*. Joann W. Kealiiohomoku, ed. Committee on Research in Dance. New York, 1970.

BrainCH   = Brainard, Ingrid. *Die Choreographie der Hoftänze in Burgund, Frankreich und Italien im 15. Jahrhundert.* Doctoral dissertation, Göttingen, 1956.

BrainRDM   = Brainard, Ingrid. "The Role of the Dancing Master in 15th Century Courtly Society," *Fifteenth Century Studies*, II (1979), 21–44.

BrainTCD   = Brainard, Ingrid. *Three Court Dances of the Early Renaissance*. New York, Dance Notation Bureau, 1971.

BukoPBDR   = Bukofzer, Manfred. "A Polyphonic Basse Dance of the Renaissance," *Studies in Medieval and Renaissance Music*. New York, Norton, 1950, 190–216.

CatCCM   = Cattin, Giulio. "Canti, Canzoni a Ballo e Danze nelle Macheronee," *Rivista Italiana di Musicologia*, X (1975), 180–215.

ClosMBD   = Closson, Ernest. *Le Manuscrit dit des Basses Danses de la Bibliothèque de Bourgogne*. Brussels, Société des Bibliophiles et Iconophiles de Belgique, 1912.

CranDBDT   = Crane, Frederick. "The Derivation of some Fifteenth Century Basse-Danse Tunes," *Acta Musicologica*, XXXVII (1965), 179–188.

CranMSBD = Crane, Frederick. *Materials for the Study of the Fifteenth Century Basse Danse*. New York, Institute of Medieval Music, 1968.

DolDSI = Dolmetsch, Mabel. *Dances of Spain and Italy from 1400 to 1600*. London, Routledge and Kegan Paul, 1954.

EitBQL = Eitner, Robert. *Biographisch-bibliographisches Quellenlexikon der Musiker und Musikgelehrten der christlichen Zeitrechnung bis zur mitte des 19. Jahrhunderts*. 10 vols. Leipzig, Breitkopf & Härtel, 1899–1904.

GalloBL = Gallo, F. Alberto. "Il Ballare Lombardo, circa 1435–1475," *Studi Musicali*, VIII (1979) 61–84.

Ghiselin, Johannes. *Collected Works*. 4 vols., ed. by Clytus Gottwald. Rome, American Institute of Musicology, 1961–1968.

GomDMM = Gombosi, Otto. "About Dance and Dance Music in the late Middle Ages," *Musical Quarterly*, XXVII (1941), 289–305.

GomCMVC = Gombosi, Otto. *Compositione di Meser Vicenzo Capirola*. Neuilly-sur-Seine, Société de Musique d'Autrefois, 1955.

Gombosi, Otto. "Der Hoftanz," *Acta Musicologica*, VII (1935), 50–61.

GomR = Gombosi, Otto. Review of *Manfred F. Bukofzer's Studies in Medieval and Renaissance Music*. New York, Norton, 1950 in *Journal of the American Musicological Society*, IV (1951), 139–147.

HeartzFCB = Heartz, Daniel. "A Fifteenth Century Ballo: Rôti Bouilli Joyeux," *Aspects of Medieval and Renaissance Music, A*

Birthday Offering to Gustave Reese, ed. by Jan La Rue. New York, Norton, 1966.

HeartzBD = Heartz, Daniel. "The Basse Dance. Its Evolution circa 1450 to 1550," *Annales Musicologiques, Moyen Age et Renaissance*, VI (1958–1963), 287–340.

HeartzHBD = Heartz, Daniel. "Hoftanz and Basse Dance," *Journal of the American Musicological Society*, XIX (1966), 13–36.

HertSBD = Hertzman, Erich. "Studien zur Basse danse im 15. Jahrhundert, mit besonderer Berücksichtigung des Brüsseler Manuskripts," *Zeitschrift für Musikwissenschaft*, XI (1929), 401–413.

HughesIM = Hughes, D.G. ed. *Instrumental Music* by Otto Kinkeldey, H.C. Robbins Landon, Eric Werner, Walter Piston. Cambridge, Mass., Harvard University Press, 1959.

JackFCB = Jackman, James L. *Fifteenth Century Basse Dances*. (The Wellesley Edition, 6) Wellesley, Mass., 1964.

JeppFROT = Jeppesen, Knud. *La Frottola III. Frottola und Volkslied: Zur musikalischen Überlieferung des folkoristischen Guts in der Frottola*. Copenhagen, 1970.

Jeppesen, Knud. "Venetian Folk-Songs of the Renaissance," Papers of the *American Musicological Society*, 1939, 69–71.

JosqWW = Josquin des Prez. *Wereldlijke Werken*, Deel II, ed. by M. Antonowycz and W. Elders, Amsterdam, 1965–1968.

KinkJD = Kinkeldey, Otto. "A Jewish Dancing Master of the Renaissance," *Studies in Jewish Bibliography and Related Subjects, in Memory of Abraham Solomon Freidus*. New York, 1929, 329–372. Reprinted as *A Jewish Dancing*

Master of the Renaissance: Guglielmo Ebreo. Brooklyn, N.Y., Dance Horizons, 1966.

LesDCD = Lesure, François. "Danses et chansons à danser au début du XVIe siècle," in *Recueil de travaux offerts à M. Clovis Brunel. (Mémoires et documents publiés par la Société de l'Ecole des Chartes*, 12). II, 176–184.

Marr-SanOAM = Marrocco, W.T. and Sandon, N. *Medieval Music.* London, Oxford University Press, 1977.

Marrocco, W.T. "Fifteenth Century Italian Dances: Ballo and Bassadanza: A Survey," *Studi Musicali* X (1981), (in press).

MarrMBT = Marrocco, W.T. "Music and Dance in Boccaccio's Time," *Part I: Fact and Speculation, Dance Research Journal*, 10/2 (1,2,–1978), 19–22.

MarrDBD = Marrocco, W.T. "The Derivation of another Bassadanza," *Acta Musicologica*, LI (1–1979), 137–139.

MazziCOR = Mazzi, Curzio. "Il 'Libro dell'arte del danzare' di Antonio Cornazano," *La Bibliofilia*, XVII (1915), 1–30.

MazziUSC = Mazzi, Curzio. "Una sconosciuta compilazione di un libro quattrocentistico di balli," *La Bibliofilia,* XVI (1914–1915), 185–209.

Melica, Ada. "Guglielmo Ebreo da Pesaro, maestro di ballo del quattrocento," *Rassegna Musicale*, XXIX (1959), 51–60.

MeyEMBD = Meylan, Raymond. *L'énigme de la musique des basses danses du 15e siècle.* Bern und Stuttgart, Publikationen der Schweizerischen Musikforschenden Gesellschaft, II, 17, 1968.

MeyRPBD   = Meylan, Raymond. "Recherche de Parentés parmi les Basses Danses du Quinzième Siècle," *Acta Musicologica*, XXXVII (1966), 46–66.

MichEDM   = Michel, Artur. "The Earliest Dance Manuals," *Medievalia et Humanistica*, III (1945), 118–129.

MotMCS   = Motta, Emilio. "Musici alla corte degli Sforza," *Archivo Storico Lombardo*, IV (1887), 29–64.

PesSRT   = Pescerelli, Beatrice. "Una sconosciuta redazione del trattato di danza di Guglielmo Ebreo," *Rivista Italiana di Musicologia,* IX (1974), 48–55.

PlamKM   = Plamenac, Dragan. *Keyboard Music of the Faenza Codex 117.* Rome, American Institute of Musicology, 1972.

PlamQSC   = Plamenac, Dragan. "Quodlibets in the Seville Chansonnier," *The Commonwealth of Music,* ed. by G. Reese and R. Brandel. New York, Free Press, 1965, 163–181.

Pope, Isabel and Kanazawa, Masakata. *The Musical Manuscript Montecassino 871.* London, Oxford University Press, 1979.

PuliOB   = Pulignani, Michele Faloci, ed. *Otto Bassedanze di M. Guglielmo da Pesaro e di M. Domenico da Ferrara, per le nozze Renier-Campostrini*, Foligno, Sgariglia, 1887.

Renier, Rodolfo, "Osservazioni sulla cronologia di un' opera del Cornazano," *Giornale Storico della letteratura Italiana,* XVII (1891), 142–146.

RonDVD   = Roncaglia, Giovanni Messori, ed. *Della virtute et arte del danzare … Trascrizione di un manoscritto inedito del XV secolo esistente nella Biblioteca Palatina di Modena …*

Pubblicata nelle nozze Tavani-Santucci. Modena, Imm. Concezione, 1885.

RossLAC = Rossi, Vittorio. *Le Lettere di Messer Andrea Calmo.* Turin, Loescher, 1888.

RossUB = Rossi, Vittorio, ed. *Un Ballo a Firenze nel 1459. Nozze Fraccaroli-Resonico.* Bergamo, Istituto Italiano d'Arti Grafiche, 1885.

Sachs, Curt. *The Commonwealth of Art: Style in the Fine Arts, Music and the Dance.* New York, Norton, 1946.

SachRT = Sachs, Curt. *Rhythm and Tempo.* New York, Norton, 1953.

SachWHD = Sachs, Curt. *World History of the Dance.* New York, Norton, 1963.

SmithBDM = Smith, Margaret Dean. "A Fifteenth Century Dancing Book," *Journal of English Folk Dance and Song Society*, III (1937), 100–110.

SoutBDM = Southern, Eileen. "Basse-Dance Music in some German Manuscripts of the 15th Century," *Aspects of Medieval and Renaissance Music, a Birthday Offering to Gustave Reese*, ed. by Jan La Rue. New York, Norton, 1966.

SoutSKBD = Southern, Eileen. "Some Keyboard Basse Dances of the Fifteenth Century," *Acta Musicologica*, XXXV (1963), 114–124.

SoutBOB = Southern, Eileen. *The Buxheim Organ Book.* (Musicological Studies, 6). Brooklyn, N.Y., Institute of Medieval Studies, 1963.

ThomMBT = Thomas, Emma Lewis. "Music in Boccaccio's Time," Part II: *Reconstruction of Danze and Balli* (including three dances with music and Labanotation), *Dance Research Journal*, 10/2 (1,2–1978), 23–42.

TorreSQ = Torrefranca, Fausto. *Il Segreto del Quattrocento*. Milan, Hoepli, 1939.

ToulABD = Toulouse, Michel. *L'art et instruction de bien dancer*. A.E. Lequet, Translator; music transcribed and edited by R. Rastall; bibliographical note by V. Scholderer, New York, Dance Horizons republication, 1951. (Facsimile copy of the Royal College of Physicians Edition, London, 1936).

VitPGG = Vitaletti, Guido. "Per la fortuna di Dante nel secolo XV. 'Il Pellegrino' di Gaugello Gaugelli (cod. Vat. Urb. 692)," *Giornale Dantesco*, XXIV (1921), 217–226.

WallBO = Wallner, B.A. *Das Buxheimer Orgelbuch*. Das Erbe Deutscher Musik, Vol. 37, pt. 1, Kassel und Basel, 1958.

Wood, Melusine. *Some Historical Dances*. London, The Imperial Society of Teachers of Dancing: C.W. Beaumont, 1952.

Young, William. "Keyboard Music to 1600," *Musica Disciplina*, XVI (1962), 115–150.

ZamTGE = Zambrini, Francesco, ed. *Trattato dell'arte del ballo di Guglielmo Ebreo Pesarese*. Bologna, Romagnoli, 1873. (Reprint: Forni, Bologna, 1968).

ZanAC = Zannoni, Giovanni. "Il 'Libro dell'arte del danzare' di Antonio Cornazano," *Rendiconti della R. Accademia dei Lincei*, Serie 4, Vol. 6, (1890), Rome.

II. Description of the Codices

The present repertoire of fifteenth century Italian dances consists of ten treatises[1] — the works of three dance masters, Domenico da Piacenza (or Ferrara) and his disciples, Antonio Cornazano and Guglielmo Ebreo da Pesaro, the last adopting the name Giovanni Ambrogio after his conversion to Christianity.[2] Established by Domenico, the format of the dance treatise consisted of an introduction in praise of the art of dance, a theoretical section explaining the requisites of a dancer such as manner, bearing, grace and the various ways in which the four dance-types, *bassadanza, quaternaria, saltarello* and *piva* are danced, and concluding with a number of choreographies of *bassedanze* and *balli,* sometimes with music.

Domenico's treatise is titled *De arte saltandi & choreas ducendi*, followed by a subtitle in Italian, *De le arte de ballare et danzare,* and is preserved in Paris, Bibliothèque Nationale, *fonds it. 972.* It was compiled by no fewer than six scribes* perhaps under the master's guidance, since it is written in the third person and refers to the master as "lo Spectabile et egregio Cavagliero Misser Domenico da Piasença." While legible, the scribes' writing skills can be described only as awkward, often obscuring the meaning of the directions.

Artur Michel suggests that Domenico was at least 35 years of age when his treatise was written about 1450 and places his birth about 1420.[3] Daniel Heartz is in agreement and adds that the treatise "contains balli with Este connections, but not suggesting Sforza connections; however, a fly-leaf inscription in Latin gives the name of the (first?) owner as 'Duke of Milan, Count of Pavia and Angera, etc.' helping to situate the MS in the latter part of the master's career, or as a compromise, somewhere between Este and Sforza service, i.e. about 1450.[4] Perhaps another clue to the date is the music notation which is similar to that of the Oxford MS, Bodleian Library, *Canonici misc. 213,* and the Trent *codex 92*, Castello del Buon Consiglio. In brief, void notes (white notation) of the early renaissance are used throughout as opposed to filled-in (black notation) of the *ars nova* period.

---

*According to Dr. Edward Tuttle, philologist and professor of Italian at the University of California, Los Angeles, who has recently completed a study of Domenico's treatise.

Domenico's manual consists of 59 paper pages measuring 245 x 180 mm. The theoretical section from f. 1r to 7r is immediately followed by choreographies of 15 *balli,* each with music. The five *bassedanze,* however, are given without music. All choreographies are by Domenico including *La Fia Guilmin,* whose music according to the first scribe, is a *ballata francese* (French ballad).

Antonio Cornazano, humanist, poet and dancing master, was born in Piacenza in 1430 and died in Ferrara in 1484. He, too, was in the service of the Sforza family in Milan and the Este in Ferrara. Among his many writings is his *Libro dell'arte del danzare,* preserved in Rome, Biblioteca Apostolica Vaticana, codex *Capponiano, 203,* in which he acknowledges Domenico as "mio solo maestro et compatriota, misser Domenichino da Piacença, cavagliero aurato per la sua perfecta et famossisima virtute" (my only master and compatriot, seignior Domenichino da Piacença, enlightened cavalier for his perfect and most famous artistry). The manual was written in 1455 for the engagement of Ippolita d'Este (who was only ten years of age) to the duke of Calabria. The Vatican library possesses a copy (dedicated to Sforza Secondo) of the now vanished 1455 manuscript, with additions by Cornazano. The manuscript carries no date, but Mazzi informs us that the answer can be deduced from the dedicatory sonnet which refers to Ippolita's trip traversing Italy to wed her betrothed in June 1465:[5]

> E cosi, riverente a' vostri piedi mando copia di quel che all' excellente vostra Sorella, intitulato diedi: I' dico di quell'una ch'al presente ha traversato Italia a tôr marito et ha el bisson d'un re facto parente.
> (And thus, reverently at your feet, I send a copy of that [treatise] dedicated to your excellent sister; I speak of that one who at present has crossed Italy to wed and has made that viper of a king a relative.)

The treatise contains 35 vellum folios, 164 x 115 mm. bound in red leather. Following the dedication to Ippolita, Duchess of Calabria, there are choreographies and music of eight *balli,* choreographies of three *bassedanze,* and the *tenori* (tenor melodies) of three other *bassedanze.* We are informed by Cornazano that the *balli* and *bassedanze* (except *La Spagna, Cançon de' pifari* and *Collinetto*) are the creations of his teacher, Domenico (f. 28v). However, these eleven dances are presented as new choreographies; the others he claims, are "o troppo vecchi o troppo divulgati" (either too old or too popularized) to be included. They are: *precicogna, Fidel ritorna, el zoioso, Leoncello in dui,*

Berreguardo in dui, Anello, Gellosia, Presoniera, Madama genevra, Marchesana, bel fiore, La Seve, Levoretta, bassadança Secreta, La Reale, Fodra e la Mignotta vecchia e con altri molti." Yet, among these one notices *balli* and *bassedanze* entered in later treatises such as *PBN 476* and in work copies *FML* and *NYPL*.

Of the three dancing masters, Guglielmo Ebreo da Pesaro appears to have travelled most extensively in Italy and testifies in the postscript of his treatise, *PBN 476* (see below), to his presence and participation at the festivities of the most sumptuous and elegant courts in Florence,[6] Bologna, Mantua, Ferrara, Pavia, Urbino, Ravenna, Padua, Forlì, Naples and Venice (where he was knighted by the Emperor (f. 69r).[7] Certainly, no other dancing master was so eagerly sought after and none other so capitalized on his advantages of being in demand. Guglielmo's treatise, perhaps his first (see below), titled, *Guglielmi Hebraei pisauriensis de pratica seu arte tripudii vulgare opusculum*, preserved in Paris, Bibliothèque Nationale, *fonds it. 973*, is dedicated to his patron, Galeazzo Sforza, and is the most beautifully limned and carefully executed of all the manuscripts, the work of the amanuensis, Paganus Raudensis (Pagano da Rho), in Milan, 1463. It consists of 57 parchment pages (including the dedication) measuring 260 x 180 mm; bound in green velvet, it is the only one of Guglielmo's manuscripts with a miniature on f. 21v of three dancers holding hands and poised as though to begin a dance to the accompaniment of a harpist shown in the background. The treatise is divided into two parts: the first from f. 1v to 21v contains the theory and a Socratic dialogue on dance containing material similar to Domenico's; the second contains the table of contents from f. 22r to 22v, the choreographies from f. 23r to 43v, and the music from 46r to 51v. This codex preserves 17 *balli* and 14 *bassedanze*, but only 12 *balli* are supplied with tunes. The creator of at least 34 choreographies (including those preserved in his other manuscripts), Guglielmo was the most prolific of the three masters.[8] A laudatory poem in his honor written by a contemporary, Giovanni Mario Filelfo (1426–1480), praises Guglielmo as a dancer and musician.[9]

The fourth manuscript, untitled, is preserved in Foligno, Seminario Vescovile, Biblioteca L. Jacobilli, *MS D.I. 42*. On paper measuring 223 x 149 mm, this fragment consists of 16 loose pages, undoubtedly the remains of a larger volume. In addition to the eight *bassedanze* choreographies on folios 1r to 4r (no music, regrettably) it contains three sonnets, notarial records and expense entries bearing the dates 1455 and 1461. As such, it may well be the earliest of Guglielmo's treatises. Possibly another bit of evidence in support of this source as his first attempt at writing a dance manual is his use of the words, *saltando* or *salti* (leaping or leaps). Where this manual reads "saltando col pie manco" (leaping with the left foot), his later manuals read, "incomminciando col pie manco" (beginning with the left foot). It would appear to this writer that after its first use in the *FBJ* source, Guglielmo replaced the term *saltando* with *incomminciando*, as perhaps a more appropriate term for the opening of a *bassadanza*. An edition of this treatise was made by Michele Faloci-Pulignani as a nuptial offering to the couple Renier-Campostrini in 1930.[10]

A fifth MS with the title, *De Praticha seu Arte Tripudii Vulgare opusculum, Ghuglielmi hebrei Pisauriensis*, is preserved in Florence, Biblioteca Nazionale Centrale, codex *Magliabecchiana-Strozziano XIX 88*. It consists of 40 paper folios measuring 215 x 145 mm, with two outer parchment pages; the binding is of red leather on wood. The first letter "L" is illuminated in gold leaf on a background of blue, red and green. Undated, the manuscript contains 17 *balli* and 17 *bassedanze* without music. The table of contents is on f. 1v–2v, the title on f. 3r.

A sixth MS with no title page is preserved in Siena, Biblioteca Comunale, codex *L.V.29*. Consisting of 114 parchment folios measuring 210 x 140 mm, (of which f. 89 to 114 are blank), leather bound on wood, this source is the largest, with 33 *balli* and 31 *bassedanze* without music. Guglielmo's name first appears on f. 21v, but on f. 5r he reveals himself as Domenico's pupil, "disciepolo e fervente imitatore del dignissimo Cavaliere misser Domenico da Ferrara" (disciple and fervent imitator of the most worthy Cavalier seignior Domenico da Ferrara). The first letter of the word *Hermonia* in the introductory sonnet is in gold leaf; chapter headings are in red ink; first letters of first words are in red and blue. The scribe of this codex must have had his thoughts on other matters, for the table of contents lists fewer *bassedanze* than are described in the section on choreographies. *Ginevera, Gelosia, Morosa, Alessandresca, Partita crudele*, and a second *Dannes* are described, but not listed in the table of contents. Three other *bassedanze* are listed in the table, but no choreographies are given. They are: *Venus*, *Lauro* and *Sole d'amore*. Of the *balli*, the first is entered as *Gioioso*, but the choreography is titled *Rotiboli*; *Berriguardo* is presented as *Riguardo* in the choreography, *Amor sguardo* as *Amoroso*, *La figlia Gugliemin* as *Foglie*; *Fortuna* is listed but no choreography is given; and *Marchisana* is choreographed but does not appear in the table of contents.

A seventh MS is preserved in Modena, Biblioteca Estense, codex *Ital. 82, a.J.9.4. (Olim VII A 82)*. It contains 30 paper folios 143 x 102 mm. and bound in red leather. Title page and author are lacking, but it is without doubt the work of Guglielmo, whose name first appears on f. 14r, and on f. 3v he claims himself a pupil of Domenico. Each chapter and main heading is written in red ink. There are 8 *balli* and 5 *bassedanze*, but no music. Though undated, Roncaglia (RonDVD, preface) suggests that the manuscript was written c. 1475 by Guglielmo of Flanders, *cantore*, who was as that time employed at the court of Ferrara as a singer and chirographer.

An eighth MS titled, *Domini Iohannis Ambrosii Pisauriensis de Pratica seu arte Tripudii Vulgare Opusculum*, is undated and preserved in Paris, Bibliothèque Nationale, *fonds it. 476*; it is easily readable and written by a scribe surely after the author's (Guglielmo's) conversion.[11] On paper and leather bound, this manuscript consists of 81 pages measuring 272 x 180 mm. The table of contents takes up f. 3r to 6r (new numbering); there follows one blank page; the title is on f. 8r; there follow two blank pages; between 8r and 32v there follows the same sonnet, *Dal ermonia suave el dolce canto*, etc., *Proemium*, the chapters on *Misura*, *Partire del terreno*, *l'Ayre*, *Maniera*, *Movimento corporeo*, the various experiments between the dancer and musician, and finally the Socratic dialogue. Here, also, the space for the illustration of the three dancers and musician was left unfilled. The choreographies begin at f. 33v and continue to 59v; there are blank pages from f. 60r to 61v; the tunes for the *balli* from f. 62r to 66r; blank but ruled pages from f. 66v to 71v; and from 72r to 80r Ambrogio's accounts of his visits to the various courts in Italy. There are 15 *bassedanze* and 20 *balli*; 17 *balli* tunes are given, but one of which, PIZOCHARA, was not supplied with a choreography.

A ninth MS with the title on f. 2r, *Guglielmus ebreis pisauriensis de praticha seu arte tripudi vorghare opusculum*, is preserved in Florence, Biblioteca Medicea-Laurenziana, codex *Antinori, A 13*. Bound in red leather, the manuscript consists of 88 pages measuring 225 x 160 mm, and is written in cursive style throughout, the work of one scribe who undoubtedly made his copy from *FBNC*. Folios 29v to 42r and 58v to 88r are lined but blank. The first and last page are of parchment taken from an eleventh century missal. There are 21 *balli* and 17 *bassedanze* all without music. Dated 6 December 1510, it is (with the *NYPL* codex) the last of the Guglielmo copies.

A tenth manuscript, *Guglielmi ebrei pisaurienses de pratica seu arte tripudi vulghare opusculum. Feliciter incipit con grolia sia iddio senper*, appears to be the work of two scribes who spelled each other at various intervals. The original owner was probably Giorgio del Giudeo who wrote on the fly-leaf:

> Questa è la copia di messer giorgio del giudeo di ballare bassedanze e balletti e questa è la tavola della composizione del ballo e di bassedanze e balletti composte per misser Domenico da Ferrara e da misser Giovanni Ambrogio che fu ebreo.
> (This is the copy belonging to Master Giorgio of the Jew [of the manner] of dancing *bassedanze* and *balletti* and this is the table [of contents] of *balli*, *bassedanze* and *balletti* choreographies composed by master Domenico da Ferrara and by Giovanni Ambrogio who was Jewish.)

It is not known who the subsequent owners were after the sixteenth century, but it came to light in this century when Walter Toscanini acquired it from the Florentine publishers, Olschki, who obtained it from Cia Fornaroli, prima ballerina of the La Scala opera house in the 1920s. Toscanini, who eventually donated the manuscript and a number of other dance manuals on microfilm to the New York Public Library, was of the opinion that the paper of this manuscript was the kind used in Tuscany about 1460 because of the similarity of its watermark with one listed in Briquet's *Les Filigranes*, I, 3387.[12] In my opinion, the addition of six new *balli* and the ascription of several dances to Giovanni Ambrogio suggests the completion of this manuscript about the end of the fifteenth century, or after his conversion to Catholicism. There are 70 pages measuring 286 x 216 mm. written at times with extreme haste, containing 22 *bassedanze*, 20 *balli* and 13 *balletti* without music. All following folio references to this source are based on Alberto Gallo's new numeration (see GalloBL).

III.   The Dances

The choreographies of 43 *bassedanze*, 44 *balli* and 7* *balletti* are preserved. The *bassadanza*, acknowledged as the queen of the measures by the dancing masters, was a formal, stately court dance with undulating movements of the body resulting from the steps rising to half toe and lowering in a forward path. This dance restricted its choreography to *movimenti naturali* (natural movements) such as *passi sempi* and *doppi, riverenze, continenze, mezze volte, contrapassi* and *riprese*, the last occasionally embellished by the modifier, *in galone*** (also *gallone*), or *in portogalese*.** The *volta del gioioso* employed in several dances also appears to have been well known by the participants in MESCHINA (*SBC*, 51v), GIOVE (SBC, 69r) and others, but the manner of execution eludes this writer. Perhaps to enliven the reserved style of the *bassadanza*, the choreography at times calls for interjections of the *saltarello*. Cornazano affirms that the *bassedanze* are "fora del vulgo fabricati per sale signorile e da esser dançati per dignissime Madonne et non plebeie" (*RBV*, f. 12v). (... not for common folk, but designed for princely halls and danced by the most noble ladies).

The *ballo*, as contrast, was a rather lively dance which permitted the performers to indulge in hops, skips and leaps. In addition to the *movimenti naturali*, measures of the *piva, quaternaria, saltarello* and *bassadanza* were interjected and such other movements called *frappamento, schossa*, (also *schossetto*), *pizzigamento, squassetto, galoppo, posata, scorsa* (also *stracorsa*) and *scambiamento* (also *scambio*)[13] all vaguely termed *movimenti accidentali* by the dancing masters, but without a word of explanation. These are, however, accessories or ornaments and are acquired according to Domenico "per accidentia" (spontaneously?, intuitively?).

Seven *balletti* are listed as such in the table of contents of this volume. However, the reader must be alerted to the disconcerting discrepancies that some *balletti* are classified as *balli* in some manuals and as *balletti* in others. (See

---

*The number varies according to sources, but see further.

**These terms are nowhere defined. They may be a more elaborate *ripresa* as found in DAPHNES (*973*, f. 28r, line 14) where Guglielmo writes, "E poi gli huomini vadano indietro con due riprese in portogalese larghe ..." (Then the men move backwards with two large [wide] *riprese* in the portuguese manner). See also PRINCIPESSA (*973*, f. 30v, line 12).

CHIRINTANA, which is entered as a *ballo* in the *SBC* table of contents, f. 61v, here spelled GIURINTANA, but as a *balletto* in the choreography, 66r. For other examples see numbers 2c, 5a, 17, 48 and 54f in this volume).

Balletto is the diminutive of *ballo* and is defined as a "piccolo e breve ballo" (small and brief *ballo*). No such distinction is made by the dancing masters, but Cornazano describes the *balletto* as follows:

> Gli ballitti [sic] sono una compositione di diverse misure che po contegnire in se tutti gli nove movimenti corporei naturali ordinato ciascun con qualche fondamento di proposito come pare della Mercantia e della Sobria che sono contrarie l'una dell'altra di sententia, cioè, che in una la donna da audientia a tutti anche se fossero ben mille, nell'altra non attende alcuno senno a colui con cui ella se prima accopiata (*RBV*, f. 7v–8r).
>
> (The *balletti* are a composition of divers measures which can contain within itself all nine corporeal natural movements each with a fundamental plan of action as appears in *Mercantia* and *Sobria* which are contrary to each other in motive, that is, where in the former the woman gives audience to all though there were a thousand, and in the latter she attends to no one except the man with whom she was first paired.)

It would appear that Cornazano first differentiated between the *ballo* and *balletto* by adding the element of a mimed plot to the latter; yet, his choreographies of MERCANTIA and SOBRIA are listed as *balli* in his manual. There are 13 *balletti* classified as such in *NYPL*, one of which, LA FORTTUNA, by Marjotto da Perugia, has its choreographic action revolving around the possessor of a ring.

The three dancing masters devote a section of their treatises to the four *misure* and their relative speeds. Domenico begins his explanation with the slowest of the dances, the *bassadanza*, and continues with the *quaternaria*, which he states is one sixth faster than the *bassadanza*; the *saltarello*, which is one sixth faster than the *quaternaria*; and the *piva*, which is half again faster than the *bassadanza* (972, f. 3r–3v). A diagram of a ladder illustrates the progression from the slow *bassadanza* to the fast *piva* (f.4v).

Arbitrarily placing the beat at about one per second (slightly slower than the heart beat), the *bassadanza* would be danced at about 60 MM, the *quaternaria* about 70, the *saltarello* about 80, and the *piva* about 90. Curt Sachs (SachRT, 204) errs in his calculations of *tempi* speeds for he states, "the *piva* was about twice as fast compared with the ceremonious, courtly *bassadanza*, the livelier *quaternaria* was at 5:6, the brisk *saltarello* as 5:8, and the full speed *piva* as 1:2 ..." This is a misinterpretation of Domenico's directions who states, "... questa mexura ultima dicta piva bene ad esser più strecta de la bassadanza tri sesti (f. 3v). (This last mentioned measure called *piva* can well be three sixths faster than the *bassadanza.* ...")

Cornazano begins with the fastest of the dances, the *piva*, and moves upwards on his ladder diagram through the *saltarello*, *quaternaria* and *bassadanza*, each measure being decreased in speed by one sixth, and of course arriving at the same conclusion, namely — the *piva* is half again faster than the *bassadanza*. What is undoubtedly a clerical error in Antonio's diagram (f. 10r) is the indication that all measures are in *perfecto maggiore* [%] save the *piva* which is given as *perfecto minore* [¾].

Guglielmo appears to have borrowed from his master, but omits the ladder diagram. He does, however, provide the reader with a sample choreography whereby the novice may try out the various dance steps, including the manner of dancing a *saltarello* and *bassadanza* in the tempo of a *quaternaria* (*SBC*, f. 33v,34r,34v, and in *MBE*, f. 20v,21r).

There is almost agreement in the duration of the *movimenti naturali*: the *mezza volta* which takes up one bar according to Guglielmo and Cornazano, but a half bar in Domenico's manual; and Cornazano does not mention the duration of the *riverenza*, nor does Domenico the duration of the three *contrapassi*.

Domenico's use of the term, *tempo*, requires clarification. In the musical terminology of the *ars nova* and *renaissance, tempo* expressed the length of the brevis which was divisible into three semibreves (three quarter notes) and labeled *perfectum*, or divisible into two semibreves and labeled *imperfectum*. One of the fourteenth century composers/theorists, Jacopo da Bologna stated, "Nota che il tempo e il breve una cosa significano"* (Take note that *tempo* and brevis signify the same thing). Therefore, the brevis had the duration of one bar of music. But Domenico gives an added meaning to *tempo*, namely, that which indicates step units. As an example of this duality,** when he directs

---

L'arte del biscanto misurato (Florence, Biblioteca Medicea-Laurenziana, codex Redi 71, f. 43r).

**I am indebted to Dr. Emma Lewis Thomas for having clarified the difference between the two units.

the dancers to execute "uno tempo per motto di bassadanza in uno tempo di quaternaria," the performers understand that they must fit one *tempo* of the *bassadanza* movement (step unit), triple time in its natural mode, into one *tempo* (time unit) of the *quaternaria*, duple time in its natural mode (see *PBN* 972, f. 6r).

All dancing masters provided detailed instructions on a very important fact, namely, that each of the measures may be danced at different speeds; the *bassadanza* and *saltarello* in five, the *quaternaria* and *piva* in four, thus imparting variety to the dances. The chart given below is my reconstruction of the directions as presented by Domenico (f. 5r–7r). However, all dancing masters admit that certain dances, when performed out of their natural mode, become "troppo largo" (too slow), such as *bassadanza* 4, *saltarello* 2, *piva* 3 and 4 or "prestissimo" (too fast) such as *saltarello* 3 and 5.

Chart of Dance Tempi

BASSADANZA O* (3/4)
♩ = c. 60 MM
Music begins on the up beat

1. Danced in its natural mode (one double step).
2. Dance 2 tempi (step units) of piva to one tempo (time unit) of bassadanza
3. Dance 1 tempo (step unit) of quaternaria to 1 tempo (time unit) of bassadanza
4. Dance 1 tempo (step unit) of saltarello to 1 tempo (time unit) of bassadanza
5. Dance 2 tempi (step units) of saltarello to 1 tempo (time unit) of bassadanza

QUATERNARIA C (2/4)
♩ = c. 70 MM
Music begins on the down beat

1. Danced in its natural mode (one double step and one *frappamento*)
2. Dance 1 tempo (step unit) of bassadanza to 1 tempo (time unit) of quaternaria
3. Dance 1 tempo (step unit) of saltarello to 1 tempo (time unit) of quaternaria
4. Dance 2 tempi (step units) of piva to 1 tempo (time unit) of quaternaria

SALTARELLO O (6/8)
♩ = c. 80 MM
Music begins on the up beat

1. Danced in its natural mode (one double step and one *salteto*)
2. Dance 2 tempi (step units) of saltarello to 1 tempo (time unit) of bassadanza
3. Dance 1 tempo (step unit) of bassadanza to 1 tempo (time unit) of saltarello
4. Dance 1 tempo (step unit) of quaternaria to 1 tempo (time unit) of saltarello
5. Dance 2 tempo (step units) of piva to 1 tempo (time unit) of saltarello

PIVA C (6/8)
♩ = c. 90 MM
Music begins on the down beat

1. Danced in its natural mode (one double step)
2. Dance 1 tempo (step unit) of bassadanza to 2 tempi (time units) of piva
3. Dance 1 tempo (step unit) of quaternaria to 2 tempi (time units) of piva
4. Dance 1 tempo (step unit) of saltarello to 2 tempi (time units) of piva

---

* According to Domenico, the *bassadanza* is danced in *mazor imperfecto* (3/4), which is its natural mode (*PBN 972*, f. 2v, 3r, 5v–5r). When introduced briefly into a *ballo*, the *bassadanza* is usually in *minore perfecto* (6/8). See the choreographies of *Belreguardo, Leonzello, Pizochara, Marchexana* and *Mercantia* and their respective melodies where the change to the *bassadanza* measure is indicated in the music by the prolation symbol ℂ.

IV.   The Music

The dance tunes for 23 *balli* and 3 *bassadanze* are included in only four sources.[14] The *bassedanze* are unica; however, there are musical concordances in some secular vocal compositions (*frottole* and *chansons*) as can be seen in Nos. 18, 33, 41, 66, 91 and 92. But the *balli* are at times duplicated in other dance manuals, often with slight rhythmic and/or melodic variations. Only the melodies are given—there is no accompaniment and no indication as to what instruments are called for or the number of instrumentalists required. However, Giovanni Ambrogio touches on these points and informs us that although the musicians all play the same dance, each performs a different "aira" (air or part). A bagpipe, organ (organetto?), lute, harp, little drum with flutes, may be used to accompany the dancers.[15] Since only one part is provided it is assumed that the other parts were improvised; two or three lower parts for the *ballo* and two or three upper parts for the *bassadanza*. To be sure the iconography of the period supports this view; musicians, usually in the background or at one side and sometimes on a balcony, are in the act of playing their instruments. Without the telltale evidence of music stands, all appear to be playing by rote. Whether or not their individual parts were indeed memorized and played with no subtle or minute changes, or each performance of the same dance was a new and spontaneous arrangement of the tune, is a problem which may never be satisfactorily solved.

All three *bassedanze tenori* (usually derived from a *chanson* or *canzona*) are notated in uniform semibreves largely stepwise in movement and modal in sound, and, as the *tenori* may be adapted to any one of the four measures, they are purposefully represented as *note senza valore* (notes without value) to allow the musicians and performers the choice of measure—duple or triple—simple or compound (*RBV*, f. 33v). These are in sharp contrast to the *balli* melodies which often appear to be cast in modes closely resembling our major and minor keys such as the Lydian with a B flat signature—our F major; Dorian—our natural D minor; Ionian—our C major.[16] The music of the *balli* is tuneful and lively, many having clear-cut four bar structure and usually with meter and tempo changes within a composition often indicated by prolation symbols.[17]

Giovanni Ambrogio touches upon music theory and informs us that there are two "chiavi" (keys) called "B molle" and "B quadro" (roughly equivalent to our minor and major scale system). The latter is "aieroso" (airy or lively), but "piu cruda e men dolcie" (crude, i.e., not refined and less sweet) and similarly every dancer must be attuned to the music in order to match his movements to the mood and sound of the music (*PBN 476*, f. 13r–13v). On this matter Domenico and Cornazano are silent.

Territorial boundaries were no obstacles to cultural exchanges, and while Italo-Gallic relations were sometimes irreparably strained, songs and dances flowed from one country to the other with apparent ease, as has been proved by *Rostiboli gioioso* and its French counterpart, *Rôti bouilli joyeux; Re di Spagna* with *Casulle le novele (Castille la nouvelle* or *Castilla la nueva), Biance flour* and *Collinetto*. Many other dance tunes have been found to be derived from *chansons* and *canzone*.[18]

V. The Choreographies

1a. ALESSANDRESCA

Choreography: Guglielmo Ebreo da Pesaro.
Dance type: *Bassadanza,* 1 M* and 1 W.*
Source:
1. *FBJ, D.I. 42;* f. 3r.
2. *FBJ, D.I. 42;* f. 3v.
Music: Not preserved.
Edition: PuliOB, 17–18.

1b. ALESSANDRESCA

Choreography: Guglielmo Ebreo da Pesaro.
Dance type: *Bassadanza,* 1 M and 1 W.
Sources:
1. *PBN, 973;* 23r,23v.
2. *FBNC, XIX 88;* f. 17r,17v.
3. *PBN, 476;* f. 33v,34r,34v.
4. *FML, A 13;* f. 18r,18v.
5. *NYPL, 72–254;* f. 13r.
Music: Not preserved.
Edition: ZamTGE, 39–41.

1c. AL[E]SANDRESCA

Choreography: Guglielmo Ebreo da Pesaro.
Dance type: *Bassadanza,* 2 M and 1 W.
Source: *SBC, L. V. 29;* f. 44r,44v,45r.
Music: Not preserved.
Remarks: There are two versions in *FBJ* differing slightly from each other, but neither corresponding exactly with those in the other sources. The unusual length of the choreography in *SBC* proved to be a scribal *lapsus.* Although retaining the title and number of dancers (*in due*), the choreography is that of

---

*M = Gentleman, W = Lady

CORONA GENTILE. Detecting his error after completing about three fourths of the choreography, the scribe switched to the choreography for ALESSANDRESCA without a word of explanation.
Edition: MazziUSC, 197–198.

2a. AMOROSO
Choreography: Ascribed to Domenico da Piacenza by Guglielmo Ebreo.*
Dance type: *Ballo*, 3 dancers.
Source: *SBC, L.V. 29;* f. 71r.
Music: Not preserved.
Edition: MazziUSC, 203.

2b. AMOROSO
Choreography: Giovanni Ambrogio?
Dance type: *Ballo,* 1 M and 1 W.
Source: *PBN, 476;* f. 58v,59r.
Music: *PBN, 476;* f. 65v.
Remarks: The dances are listed as having been composed by Messere Domenico and by Messere Giovanni Ambrogio and each entry is indeed ascribed to one or the other except the three dances described as *francese* of which the present is one and unascribed.
Edition: HughesIM, 89–90.**

2c. AMOROSO
Choreography: Giovanni Ambrogio.
Dance type: *Balletto,* 1 M and 1 W.
Source: *NYPL, 72–254;* f. 29v.
Music: Not preserved.
Edition: None.

---

*Guglielmo Ebreo: abbreviated form used here for choreographies ascribed by Guglielmo Ebreo da Pesaro to others.
** This edition refers only to the music transcribed into modern notation by Otto Kinkeldey.

3. AMOROSO ISGHUARDO

Choreography: Presumably by Guglielmo/Giovanni.
Dance type: *Balletto,* 1 M and 1 W.
Source: *NYPL, 72–254;* f. 27v.
Music: Not preserved.
Edition: None.

4a. ANELLO

Choreography: Domenico da Piacenza.
Dance type: *Ballo,* 2 M and 2 W.
Sources:
1. *PBN, 972;* f. 16r,16v.
2. *PBN, 973;* f. 39r,39v.
3. *FBNC, XIX 88;* f. 35v,36r.
4. *PBN, 476;* f. 51v,52r,52v.
5. *FML, A 13;* f. 49v, 50r.
6. *NYPL, 72–254;* f. 21r.
Music: *PBN, 972;* f. 16r.
Editions: BianchiT, 135–136; HughesIM, 90–91; ZamTGE, 93–35.

4b. ANELLO

Choreography: Ascribed to Domenico da Piacenza by Guglielmo Ebreo.
Dance type: *Ballo,* 2 M and 2 W.
Sources:
1. *SBC, L.V. 29;* f. 72r,72v.
2. *MBE, Ital. 82. a.J.9.4;* f. 25v,26r.
Music: Not preserved.
Remarks: All sources acknowledge Domenico as the creator of the choreography except *NYPL* which has no ascription. Guglielmo retained the title and the initial opening—8 *tempi of saltarello*—then continued with a new choreography. Mentioned in RossLAC, 232 and 293.
Edition: RonDVD, 41.

5a.   ANGELOSA
Choreography: Ascribed to Domenico da Piacenza by Guglielmo Ebreo.
Dance type: *Ballo,* 1 M and 1 W.
Source: *SBC, L.V. 29;* f. 64v,65r,65v.
Music: Not preserved.
Remarks: Classified as *ballo* in rubric, as *balletto* in choreography.
Edition: MazziUSC, 202.

5b.   ANGELOSA
Choreography: No ascription.
Dance type: *Balletto,* 1 M and 1 W.
Source: *NYPL, 72–254;* f. 29v,30r.
Music: Not preserved.
Remarks: Title entered as RANGELOSA in GalloBL, 76.
Edition: None.

6.   ANGIOLA
Choreography: Ascribed to Domenico da Piacenza by Guglielmo Ebreo.
Dance type: *Ballo,* 2 M and 1 W *à la fila* (single file, facing the same direction).
Source: *SBC, L.V. 29;* f. 75r,75v,76r.
Music: Not preserved.
Remarks: Perhaps the same *ballo* as L'ANGIOLA BELLA performed in Florence's *piazza Santa Croce* to celebrate the presence of Pope Pius II in that city the end of April and the first days of May, 1459. (See RossUB, 16.)
Edition: MazziUSC, 205.

7.   AYS
Choreography: Ascribed to Domenico da Piacenza by Guglielmo Ebreo.
Dance type: *Bassadanza,* 2 M and 1 W.
Source: *SBC, L.V. 29;* f. 38r,38v,39r.
Music: Not preserved.
Remarks: See CATERVA.
Edition: MazziUSC, 194.

8. BASSA DI CASTIGLIA, LA

Choreography: Presumably by Guglielmo Ebreo da Pesaro.
Dance type: *Bassadanza,* 1 M and 1 W.
Source: *FML, A 13;* f. 28v,29r.
Music: Perhaps danced to the music of RE DI SPAGNA.
Remarks: LA BASSA DI CASTIGLIA and LA SPAGNA are *bassedanze* which differ considerably; LA SPAGNA is rather short, having only 21 steps as opposed to 90 in LA BASSA CASTIGLIA, which has its choreography divided into three parts of unequal lengths. Although no music is given for either dance, it is assumed that they are related to or may share the same *bassadanza* tenor as RE DI SPAGNA, which appears as music only with no choreography in *RBV 32r,32v.*
Editions: BukoPBDR,199–200; Marr-SanOAM, 238.

9. BASSA FRANZESSE

Choreography: Presumably by Guglielmo Ebreo da Pesaro.
Dance type: *Bassadanza,* 1 M and 1 W.
Source: *NYPL, 72–254;* f. 31r.
Music: Not preserved.
Remarks: This *bassadanza* contains two *riprese franzesse*, which presume executing the steps as they are described in ToulABD rather than in the Italian manner described in BrainTCD.
Edition: None.

10. BEL FIORE

Choreography: Domenico da Piacenza.
Dance type: *Ballo,* 2 M and 1 W.
Sources:
1. *PBN, 972;* f. 15r,15v.
2. *PBN, 973;* f. 37v,38r.
3. *FBNC, XIX 88;* f. 34r,34v.
4. *SBC, L.V. 29;* f. 87r,87v.
5. *PBN, 476;* f. 50r,50v.
6. *FML, A 13;* f. 48r,48v.
7. *NYPL, 72–254;* f. 20r.

Music: *PBN, 972;* f. 15r.
Remarks: Guglielmo retained Domenico's title, but made several minor changes, such as replacing his master's generic term *movimento* with a more specific term *scossetto*, substituting three tempi of *piva* for Domenico's four etc. A piece bearing the title, *Bel fiore dança* appears in other non-dance codices, but there is no similarity with Domenico's music. (See PlamKM, No. 36.) It is mentioned in TorreSQ, 81.
Editions: BianchiT, 134–135; HughesIM, 91–92; ZamTGE, 89–90.

11a.   BEL REGUARDO

Choreography: Domenico da Piacenza.
Dance type: *Ballo,* 1 M and 1 W.
Source: *PBN, 972;* f. 7v.
Music: PBN, 972; f. 7v.
Remarks: This *ballo* is mentioned in RossUB, 16.
Editions: BianchiT, 122–124; BrainCH, 313–316; HughesIM, 92–94.

11b.   BEL REGUARDO *nuovo* (new)

Choreography: Domenico da Piacenza.
Dance type: *Ballo,* 2 M and 1 W.
Source: *PBN, 972;* f. 8r,8v.
Music: *PBN, 972;* f. 7v.
Editions: BianchiT, 124–125; BrainCH, 317–320; HughesIM, 92–94.

11c.   BEL RIGUARDO

Choreography: Ascribed to Domenico da Piacenza by Guglielmo Ebreo.
Dance type: *Ballo,* 1 M and 1 W.
Sources:
1. *PBN, 973;* f. 40r,40v.
2. *FBNC, XIX 88;* f. 37r.
3. *PBN, 476;* f. 53r,53v.
4. *FML, A 13;* f. 50v,51r.
Music:
1. *PBN, 973;* f. 46v.
2. *PBN, 476;* f. 63v.

Editions: HughesIM, 92–94; ZamTGE, 97–98; Facs: KinkJD, Reprint supplement, 45.

11d.   BEL RIGUARDO
Choreography: Unascribed, but presumably by Guglielmo Ebreo.
Dance type: *Ballo,* 1 M and 1 W.
Source: *MBE, Ital. 82, a.J.9.4;* f. 24r,24v.
Music: Not preserved.
Edition: RonDVD, 39.

11e.   BENGHUARDO
Choreography: Giovanni Ambrogio.
Dance type: *Balletto,* 1 M and 1 W.
Source: *NYPL, 72–254;* f. 26v.
Music: Not preserved.
Edition: None.

11f.   BEREGUARDO *nuovo*
Choreography: Antonio Cornazano.
Dance type: *Ballo,* 2 M and 1 W.
Source: *RBV, C 203;* f. 19r,19v,20r.
Music: *RBV, C 203;* f. 18r,18v.
Edition: MazziCOR, 20–21.

11g.   BERRIGUARDO
Choreography: Ascribed to Domenico da Piacenza in rubric (*SBC,* f. 62r) but unascribed in choreography.
Dance type: *Ballo,* 2 M and 1 W.
Sources:
1. *SBC, L.V. 29;* f. 80r,80v,81r.
2. *MBE, Ital. 82, a.J.9.4;* f. 27v,28r,28v (BEL RIGUARDO).
Music: Not preserved.
Edition: RonDVD, 43–44.

11h.   RIGUARDO

Choreography: Ascribed to Domenico da Piacenza in rubric (*SBC;* f. 62r), but unascribed on f. 63v.
Dance type: *Ballo,* 1 M and 1 W.
Sources:
1. *SBC, L.V. 29;* f. 63v.
2. *NYPL, 72–254;* f. 22v,23r (BONGHUARDO).
Music: Not preserved.
Remarks: In spite of such differences in *NYPL* as title, BONGHUARDO and Giovanni Ambrogio as choreographer, both MSS are for the most part identical.
Edition: None.

12.   BIALTE [BELTÀ?] DI CHASTIGLIA

Choreography: Presumably by Guglielmo/Giovanni.
Dance type: *Balletto,* 2 M and 1 W.
Source: *NYPL, 72–254;* f. 28v,29r.
Music: Not preserved.
Edition: None.

13.   BORGES

Choreography: Giovanni Ambrogio.
Dance type: *Bassadanza,* 2 dancers.
Source: *PBN, 476;* f. 43v.
Music: Not preserved.
Remarks: Listed as a *bassadanza Francese.*
Edition: None.

14.   CANÇON DE' PIFARI DICTO EL FERRARESE
(See music page 57).

Remarks: See ThomMBT, 29–33 for a reconstruction of the *bassadanza,* MIGNOTTA (No. 62a) in Labanotation and arranged to be danced to a harmonized version of the *bassadanza* tenor, CANÇON DE' PIFARI in MarrMBT, 39.

15. CASTELANA

Choreography: Guglielmo Ebreo da Pesaro.
Dance type: *Bassadanza,* 1 M and 1 W.
Source: *NYPL, 72–254;* f. 16v,17r.
Music: Not preserved.
Edition: None.

16a. CATERVA (CHATERVA, CATERINA)

Choreography: Guglielmo Ebreo da Pesaro.
Dance type: *Bassadanza,* 3 dancers.
Sources:
1. *PBN, 973;* f. 31r,31v.
2. *FBNC, XIX 88;* f. 27v,28r,28v.
3. *PBN, 476;* f. 42v,43r.
4. *FML, A 13;* f. 27v,28r,28v.
5. *NYPL, 72–254;* f. 12v.
Music: Not preserved.
Remarks: All MSS are in complete agreement with one another. There appears to be a tenuous connection between CATERVA AND AYS (also spelled ALIIS) since in *FBNC, FML* and *NYPL,* the title reads *AYS nominata CATERVA.* A collation of the two choreographies, however, shows no similarities. To compound the confusion, *SBC* preserves choreographies for both AYS AND CATERVA—neither corresponding to those in the abovementioned sources. *FBNC* and *FML* ascribe the choreography to Guglielmo in Bologna; *PBN 973* and *NYPL* list only Guglielmo and *PBN 476* gives Giovanni Ambrogio.
Edition: ZamTGE, 70–72.

16b. CHATERVA

Choreography: Giulio in Bologna.
Dance type: *Bassadanza,* 3 dancers.
Source: *SBC, L.V. 29;* f. 48r,48v,49r.
Music: Not preserved.
Edition: None.

17.   CHIRINTANA
Choreography: Ascribed to Domenico da Piacenza by Guglielmo Ebreo.
Dance type: *Ballo,* 6 couples. (Entered as a *ballo* in table of contents, as *ballecto* in choreography.)
Source: *SBC, L.V. 29;* f. 66v,67r.
Music: Not preserved.
Remarks: This *ballo,* described as "molto ornato" (very ornate), was performed in Florence's *piazza Santa Croce* to celebrate the presence of Pope Pius II in that city. (See RossUB, 16.)
Edition: MazziUSC, 202.

18.   COLLINETTO   (See music, page 58)

19.   COLONNESE (also CHELLONESE, CHONDOMESE, CHOLOMNESE)
Choreography: Guglielmo Ebreo da Pesaro.
Dance type: *Ballo,* 3 couples.
Sources:
1. *PBN, 973;* f. 34r,34v.
2. *FBNC, XIX 88;* f. 30v,31r,31v.
3. *SBC, L.V. 29;* f. 83v,84r,84v.
4. *PBN, 476;* f. 46r,46v,47r.
5. *FML, A 13;* f. 44v,45r.
6. *NYPL, 72–254;* f. 19v.
Music:
1. *PBN, 973;* f. 50v,51r.
2. *PBN, 476;* f. 64v.
Remarks: All sources in agreement with one another. The spelling of the *ballo* in *FML* is COLAMES, an obvious scribal *lapsus calami,* as is the opening—6 tempi of *saltarello* in lieu of 16. *SBC* is the only source which contains a dedication, "Facta per Madonna Sveva di chasa Colonna." Sveva was Alessandro's wife of a second marriage. *PBN 476* and *NYPL* ascribe the choreography to Giovanni Ambrogio.
Editions: HughesIM, 95–97; ZamTGE, 79–81; Facs: KinkJD, Reprint supplement, English translation of choreography, 20, music, 46.

20. CONSOLATA

Choreography: Ascribed to Phylippo by Guglielmo Ebreo.
Dance type: *Bassadanza,* 2 M and 2 W.
Source: *SBC, L.V. 29;* f. 53r,53v,54r.
Music: Not preserved.
Edition: MazziUSC, 199.

21. CORONA

Choreography: Domenico da Piacenza.
Dance type: *Bassadanza,* and number of dancers *à la fila.*
Sources:
1. *PBN, 972;* f. 27r.
2. *RBV, C 203;* f. 31r,31v,32r.
Music: Not preserved.
Remarks: Both choreographies are in agreement. *RBV* has no ascription.
Editions: BianchiT, 149; MazziCOR, 28; ZanAC, 291.

22a. CORONA GENTILE

Choreography: Ascribed to Domenico da Piacenza by Guglielmo Ebreo.
Dance type: *Bassadanza,* 2 M and 1 W.
Source: *SBC, L.V. 29;* f. 42v,43r,43v.
Music: Not preserved.
Edition: MazziUSC, 197.

22b. CORONA GENTILE

Choreography: Giovanni Ambrogio.
Dance type: *Bassadanza,* 4 couples.
Source: *NYPL, 72–254;* f. 15v,16r,16v.
Music: Not preserved.
Edition: None.

23. CORTA

Choreography: Ascribed to Domenico da Ferrara by Guglielmo Ebreo.
Dance type: *Bassadanza,* 2 dancers.

Source: *SBC, L.V. 29;* f. 35v,36r.
Music: Not preserved.
Edition: MazziUSC, 193.

24.   CRUDELE
Choreography: Guglielmo Ebreo da Pesaro.
Dance type: *Bassadanza,* 2 M and 1 W.
Source: *FBJ, D.I. 42;* f. 2r.
Music: Not preserved.
Edition: PuliOB, 15.

25.   CUPIDO
Choreography: Guglielmo Ebreo da Pesaro.
Dance type: *Bassadanza, à la fila.*
Sources:
1. *PBN, 973;* f. 25v,26r.
2. *FBNC, XIX 88;* f. 19v,20r.
3. *SBC, L.V. 29;* f. 50r,50v.
4. *PBN, 476;* f. 36v,37r,37v.
5. *FML, A 13;* f. 20r,20v.
6. *NYPL, 72–254;* f. 9v.
Music: Not preserved.
Remarks: All sources are in agreement with one another save *SBC,* which differs slightly. The number of participants vary from three to six, but all are "à la fila." This *bassadanza* is mentioned in RossLAC, 420.
Edition: ZamTGE, 47–48.

26.   DAMNES (also DANNES, DAMPNES, DAPHNES)
Choreography: Domenico da Piacenza.
Dance type: *Bassadanza,* 2 M and 1 W.
Sources:
1. *PBN, 972;* f. 26r,26v.
2. *PBN, 973;* f. 27v,28r,28v.
3. *RBV, C 203;* f. 30r,30v,31r.

4. *FBNC, XIX 88;* f. 21v,22r,22v.
5. *SBC, L.V. 29;* f. 57v,58r,58v,59r. (first version)
6. *SBC, L.V. 29;* f. 59v,60r,60v,61r. (second version)
7. *MBE, Ital. 82, a.J.9.4;* f. 23v,24r.
8. *PBN, 476;* f. 39r,39v,40r.
9. *FML, A 13;* f. 22r,22v,23r.
10 *NYPL, 72–254;* f. 13v,14r.
Music: Not preserved.
Remarks: Guglielmo's versions are based on Domenico's choreography, but with minor variations which have been incorporated in *PBN 973, 476, FBNC, SBC* (second version), *FML* and *NYPL. SBC* (first version) and *MBE* are similar; *RBV* appears to be an abridged version of Domenico's.
Editions: BianchiT, 147–148. Bianchi misreads the title, DAMNES, for ANNOTA, but gives the choreography for DAMNES and states, "Descrive però il Cornazano, Dannes, di cui Domenico non si preoccupò" p. 113. (Cornazano describes *Dannes,* of which Domenico did not concern himself)[!]; MazziCOR, 27–28; RonDVD, 38; ZamTGE, 52–55.

27. DANZA DI RE
Choreography: Ascribed to Domenico da Piacenza by Guglielmo Ebreo.
Dance type: *Ballo,* 2 M and 1 W.
Source: *SBC, L.V. 29;* f. 76r,76v.
Music: Not preserved.
Remarks: This *ballo* was performed in Florence's *piazza Santa Croce* to celebrate the presence of Pope Pius II in that city. (See RossUB, 16.)
Edition: MazziUSC, 205–206.

28. DIAMANTE
Choreography: Ascribed to Domenico da Piacenza by Guglielmo Ebreo.
Dance type: *Bassadanza,* 2 M and 1 W.
Sources:
1. *SBC, L.V. 29;* f. 54r,54v.
2. *MBE, Ital. 82, a.J.9.4;* f. 22r,22v.
3. *NYPL, 72–254;* f. 17r,17v.

Music: Not preserved.
Remarks: *SBC* and *MBE* are in agreement with each other, but *NYPL* has significant choreographic changes.
Edition: RonDVD, 36.

29.   DUCHESCHO

Choreography: Ascribed to Domenico da Piacenza by Guglielmo Ebreo.
Dance type: *Ballo,* 2 M and 1 W *à la fila.*
Sources:
1. *PBN, 973;* f. 32v,33r.
2. *FBNC, XIX 88;* f. 29r,29v,30r.
3. *SBC, L.V. 29;* f. 81r,81v,82r.
4. *PBN, 476;* f. 44v,45r.
5. *FML, A 13;* f. 43r,43v,44r.
6. *NYPL, 72–254;* f. 18v.
Music: Not preserved.
Remarks: All sources are in agreement save *SBC* which has minor choreographic differences. All acknowledge Guglielmo as the choreographer, but *PBN 476* gives Giovanni Ambrogio. The ballo is erroneously given as ANGELOSO (GalloBL, 75).
Edition: ZamTGE, 74–76.

30.   DUCHESSA

Choreography: Ascribed to Domenico da Piacenza by Guglielmo Ebreo.
Dance type: *Bassadanza,* 2 M and 1 W.
Sources:
1. *SBC, L.V. 29;* f. 54v,55r,55v,56r.
2. *MBE, Ital. 82, a.J.9.4;* f. 22v,23r,23v.
Music: Not preserved.
Remarks: Both MSS are in agreement with each other. *MBE* has no ascription.
Edition: RonDVD, 36–37.

31. FEBUS (also PHOEBUS, PHEBUS)
Choreography: Ascribed to Domenico da Piacenza by Guglielmo Ebreo.
Dance type: *Bassadanza,* 1 M and 2 W.
Sources:
1. *FBJ, D.I. 42;* f. 4v.
2. *PBN, 973;* f. 27r,27v.
3. *FBNC, XIX 88;* f. 21r,21v.
4. *SBC, L.V. 29;* f. 49r,49v,50r.
5. *PBN, 476;* f. 38r,38v,39r.
6. *FML, A 13;* f. 21v,22r.
7. *NYPL, 72–254;* f. 13v.
Music: Not preserved.
Remarks: All MSS in agreement with one another, save *FBJ,* which, while retaining the framework, inserts different steps and *salti,* as well as the *volta del gioioso,* not used in the other sources. *SBC* ascribes the choreography to Misser A....
Editions: PuliOB, 19; ZamTGE, 50–52.

32. FERRETRA
Choreography: Ascribed to Domenico da Piacenza by Guglielmo Ebreo.
Dance type: *Ballo,* 2 dancers.
Source: *SBC, L.V. 29;* f. 74r,74v.
Music: Not preserved.
Edition: MazziUSC, 204–205.

33a. FIA GUILMIN, LA (first version)
Choreography: Domenico da Piacenza.
Dance type: *Ballo,* 2 M and 2 W in couples.
Source: *PBN, 972;* f. 19r,19v,20r.
Music: *PBN, 972;* f. 18v,19r.
Edition: BianchiT, 139–141; HughesIM., 97–100.

33b.   FIA GUIELMINA, LA (second version)
Choreography: Domenico da Piacenza.
Dance type: *Ballo,* 1 M and 1 W.
Source: *PBN, f. 972;* f. 20r,20v.
Music: *PBN, 972;* f. 18v,19r.
Remarks: A *frottola* with the incipit, *Helas la Fille Guillemen,* is found in Ottaviano Petrucci's *Frottole libro terzo,* Venice, 1504, 53v,54r. (See also JeppFROT, 17–18.) The music of the *frottola* is identical to that of Domenico's. The melody appears again serving as the tenor to a bi-textual *chanson à* 3 with the incipits, *A Florence la ioyose cite—Ellas la fille guillemin.* (See Pope-Kanazawa, *The Musical Manuscript Montecassino 871,* 119–122 and 557–561; and Appendix I, 531–533, by Ingrid Brainard; and in a cento where the eight initial notes of the theme are interpolated in the *quodlibet, Mon seul plaisir—La dolour* (see PlamQSC, 166–167, 180.
Edition: BianchiT, 141–142.

33c.   FIGLIA GUILIELMINO (first version)
Choreography: Antonio Cornazano.
Dance type: *Ballo,* 1 M and 1 W.
Source: *RBV, C 203;* f. 23r,23v,24r.
Music: *RBV, C 203;* f. 22r,22v,23r.
Edition: MazziCOR, 22–24; ZanAC, 289.

33d.   BE'FIGLIE GUILIELMIN (second version)
Choreography: Antonio Cornazano.
Dance type: *Ballo,* 2 M and 2 W in couples.
Source: *RBV, C 203;* f. 24r,24v,25r,25v.
Music: *RBV, C 203,* f. 22r,22v,23r.
Editions: MazziCOR, 24–25; ZanAC, 289.

33e.   FIGLIA GUGLIEMIN, LA
Choreography: Guglielmo Ebreo da Pesaro.
Dance type: *Ballo,* 1 M and 1 W or 2 couples.

Sources:
1. *SBC, L.V. 29;* f. 85r,85v,86r. (Titled *Foglie di Guglielmo.*)
2. *MBE, Ital. 82, a.J.9.4;* f. 28v,29r. (1 couple)
Music: Not preserved.
Remarks: In *SBC* the ballo is titled, FOGLIE. MazziUSC, 207, presented it as a new choreography, unmindful of the scribal spelling error—*foglie* for *figlia.* It is also listed as *Foglie* in GalloBL, 72.
Editions: MazziUSC, 207; RonDVD, 44–45.

34.   FIORE DE VERTÙ
Choreography: Giovanni Ambrogio.
Dance type: *Ballo,* 2 couples.
Source: *PBN, 476;* f. 58r,58v.
Music: Not preserved.
Edition: None.

35.   FIORETTO
Choreography: Ascribed to Domenico da Piacenza by Guglielmo Ebreo.
Dance type: *Ballo,* 2 M and 1 W.
Sources:
1. *SBC, L.V. 29;* f. 74v,75r.
2. *MBE, Ital. 82, a.J.9.4;* f. 26r.
3. *NYPL, 72–254;* f. 25v.(1 M and 1 W, *Balletto.*)
Music: Not preserved.
Edition: RonDVD, 41.

36.   FLANDESCHA (also FLANDESCA, FRANDESCHA)
Choreography: Ascribed to Domenico da Piacenza by Guglielmo Ebreo.
Dance type: *Bassadanza,* 1 M and 1 W.
Sources:
1. *PBN, 973;* f. 30r,30v.
2. *FBNC, XIX 88;* f. 24r,24v.
3. *SBC, L.V. 29;* f. 47r.
4. *PBN, 476;* f. 41v.

5. *FML, A 13*; f. 24r,24v.
6. *NYPL, 72–254*; f. 11v.
Music: Not preserved.
Remarks: All sources in substantial agreement. *PBN, 973* gives Domenico as the choreographer; *NYPL* ascribes it to Guglielmo; *FBNC* and *FML* have no ascription. This *bassadanza* is mentioned in RossLAC, 420.
Edition: ZamTGE, 59–60.

37.   FODRA

Choreography: Ascribed to Domenico da Piacenza by Guglielmo Ebreo.
Dance type: *Bassadanza,* 1 M and 1 W.
Source: *SBC, L.V. 29*; f. 41r,41v,42r.
Music: Not preserved.
Edition: MazziUSC, 196.

38.   FOGLIE   (See FIGLIA GUGLIEMIN, LA   No. 33e)

Remarks: The title of this ballo is a scribal error. It is entered as FOGLIE in the choreography and as LA FIGLIA GUGLIEMIN in the *SBC* table of contents, but the choreographies (including *MBE*) are identical.

39.   FORTTUNA, LA

Choreography: Marjotto da Perugia.
Dance type: *Balletto,* 2 M and 1 W.
Source: *NYPL, 72–254*; f. 27v.
Music: Not preserved.
Remarks: The *balletto* is mentioned in RossLAC, 420. Nothing is known of the choreographer.
Edition: None.

40.   FORTUNOSA

Choreography: Domenico da Ferrara (Piacenza).
Dance type: *Bassadanza,* 2 M and 2 W.

Source: *NYPL, 72–254;* f. 17v,17r.
Music: Not preserved.
Edition: None.

41.   FRANCO CUORE GENTILE

Choreography: Ascribed to Domenico da Piacenza by Guglielmo Ebreo.
Dance type: *Ballo,* 1 M and 1 W.
Source: *SBC, L. V. 29;* f. 73v,74r.
Music: Not preserved.
Remarks: Frederick Crane states, "Although the music of *Franco cuore gentile* is not preserved, the title is too similar to that of Dufay's three part rondeau, *Franc cuer gentil, sur toutes gracieuse,* to leave doubt that the *ballo* tune was derived from the *chanson*" (CranDBDT, 183).
Edition: MazziUSC, 204.

42.   FRASA MJGNJON FRANCESSE

Choreography: Presumably by Guglielmo/Giovanni.
Dance type: *Ballo,* 1 M and 1 W.
Source: *NYPL, 72–254;* f. 31r.
Music: Not preserved.
Edition: None.

43a.   GILOXIA, LA (also GELOSIA, GIELOSIA)

Choreography: Domenico da Piacenza.
Dance type: *Ballo,* 3, 4, 5, couples.
Source: *PBN, 972;* f. 11r,11v.
Music: *PBN, 972;* f. 11r.
Editions: BianchiT, 127–128; BrainCH, 335–340.

43b.   GELOSIA (also GIELOSIA)

Choreography: Ascribed to Domenico da Piacenza by Guglielmo Ebreo.
Dance type: *Ballo,* 3, 4, 5 couples.

Sources:
1. *PBN, 973;* f. 39v,40r.
2. *FBNC, XIX 88;* f. 36r,36v,37r.
3. *SBC, L.V. 29;* f. 39r,39v,40r.
4. *MBE, Ital. 82 a.J.9.4;* f. 24v,25r.
5. *PBN, 476;* f. 52v,53r.
6. *FML. A 13;* f. 50r,50v.

Music:
1. *PBN, 973;* f. 47v,48r.
2. *PBN, 476;* f, 63r.

Remarks: For a harmonized version of this *ballo* and an English translation of the choreography see DolDSI, 164–168; VitPGG, 199.

Editions: HughesIM, 100–101; RonDVD, 39; ZamTGE, 95–96.

43c.   GELOSIA

Choreography: Domenico da Ferrara che fu ebreo (who was Jewish[!]).
Dance type: *Ballo,* 3 couples.
Source: *NYPL, 72–254;* f. 23r.
Music: Not preserved.
Remarks: This source retains the framework, but the many differences call for a separate entry.
Edition: None.

43d.   GELOSIA

Choreography: Ascribed to Domenico da Piacenza by Guglielmo Ebreo.
Dance type: *Ballo,* 3, 4, 5 couples.
Source: *SBC, L.V. 29;* f. 65v,66r.
Music: Perhaps danced to *PBN 973* or *476.*
Edition: None.

44.   GENEVRA (also GINEVRA, GENEVERA, ZINEVRA)

Choreography: Guglielmo Ebreo da Pesaro.
Dance type: *Bassadanza,* 1 M and 1 W.

Sources:
1. *PBN, 973;* f. 23v,24r,24v.
2. *FBNC, XIX 88;* f. 17v,18r,18v.
3. *SBC, L.V. 29;* f. 36v,37r. (Ascribed to Domenico.)
4. *PBN, 476;* f. 34v,35r,35v.
5. *FML, A 13;* f. 18v,19r.
6. *NYPL, 72–254;* f. 15r,15v.

Music: Not preserved.

Remarks: *PBN 973* and *476* are in agreement with each other; *FBNC* and *FML* agree with each other, but differ slightly from the above two. *NYPL* contains steps not employed by the other manuscripts. Guglielmo may have named and dedicated this *bassadanza* in honor of Ginevra, daughter of Alessandro Sforza of Pesaro. The *bassadanza* is mentioned in RossLAC, 420. The *SBC* entry on f. 36v is lacking in GalloBL, 70.

Edition: ZamTGE, 41–43.

45. GIOIA

Choreography: Ascribed to Domenico da Piacenza by Guglielmo Ebreo.
Dance type: *Bassadanza,* 2 M and 1 W.
Source: *SBC, L.V. 29;* f. 40r,40v,41r.
Music: Not Preserved.
Edition: MazziUSC, 195.

46. GIOLIVA (also GULIVA, GIULIVA, GIOLIA, GLORIA)

Choreography: Ascribed to Domenico da Piacenza by Guglielmo Ebreo.
Dance type: *Bassadanza,* 1 M and 1 W.
Sources:
1. *FBJ, D.I. 42;* f. 2v.
2. *PBN, 973;* f. 28v,29r.
3. *FBNC, XIX 88;* f. 22v,23r.
4. *SBC, L.V. 29;* f. 52r,52v,53r.
5. *PBN, 476;* f. 40r,40v.
6. *FML, A 13;* f. 23r,23v.
7. *NYPL, 72–254;* f. 11r.

Music: Not preserved.

Remarks: Only *SBC* ascribes this *bassadanza* to Domenico. All other MSS, save *FBJ,* which carries no ascription, and *PBN, 476,* which ascribes it to Giovanni Ambrogio, give Guglielmo as choreographer. *FBJ, FBNC* and *FML* are similar to *PBN, 973* with minor variations, but *SBC* and *NYPL,* while retaining the framework, are revised. MazziUSC, 186, fn.1. errs in the reading of the title in *FBJ* which he interprets as GLORIA rather than GIOLIVA or GIOLIA.

Editions: PuliOB, 16; ZamTGE, 55–57.

47.   GOJOSO SPANGNUOLO

Choreography: Presumably by Guglielmo/Giovanni.
Dance type: *Ballo,* 1 M and 1 W.
Source: *NYPL, 72–254;* f. 31r,31v.
Music: Not preserved.
Edition: None.

48a.   GRATIOSO (also GRAZIOSA, GRACIOSO, GRATIOZO)

Choreography: Ascribed to Domenico da Piacenza by Guglielmo Ebreo.
Dance type: *Ballo,* 1 M and 1 W.
Sources:
1. *PBN, 973;* f. 42r,42v.
2. *FBNC, XIX 88;* f. 37r,37v,38r.
3. *PBN, 476;* f. 55v,56r.
4. *FML, A 13;* f. 51r,51v,52r.
5. *NYPL, 72–254;* f. 22v.
Music:
1. *PBN, 973;* f. 50v.
2. *PBN, 476;* f. 62v.
Remarks: *PBN, 476* and *NYPL* ascribe the *ballo* to Giovanni Ambrogio.
Editions: HughesIM, 110–111; ZamTGE, 98-100; Facs. KinkJD, Reprint supplement, 46.

48b.   GRATIOSA, LA

Choreography: Ascribed to Domenico da Piacenza by Guglielmo Ebreo.
Dance type: *Ballo,* 1 M and 1 W.

Source: *SBC, L.V. 29;* f. 67r,67v.
Music: Not preserved.
Edition: None.

48c.   GRAZIOSA, LA

Choreography: Presumably by Guglielmo/Giovanni.
Dance type: *Balletto,* 2 M and 1 W.
Source: *NYPL, 72–254;* f. 27r.
Music: Not preserved.
Edition: None.

49.   HUMANA

Choreography: Ascribed to Domenico da Piacenza by Guglielmo Ebreo.
Dance type: *Ballo,* 2 M and 1 W.
Source: *SBC, L.V. 29;* f. 77r,77v.
Music: Not preserved.
Edition: MazziUSC, 206.

50a.   INGRATA, LA

Choreography: Domenico da Piacenza.
Dance type: *Ballo,* 2 M and 1 W.
Sources:
1. *PBN, 972;* f. 10r,10v,11r.
2. *PBN, 973;* f. 38r,38v,39r.
3. *FBNC, XIX 88;* f. 34v,35r,35v.
4. *PBN, 476;* f. 50v,51r,51v.
5. *FML, A 13;* f. 48v,49r,49v.
6. *NYPL, 72–254;* f. 20v.
Music:
1. *PBN, 972;* f. 10r.
2. *PBN, 973;* f. 48v,49r.
3. *PBN, 476;* f. 64r.
Remarks: Guglielmo retained the first section of Domenico's choreography, then continued with a new one yet adhering to the theme of the rejected suitor.

All of Guglielmo's MSS are in agreement with one another save *SBC* (below). **Editions:** BianchiT, 126–127; HughesIM, 110–114; Marr-SanOAM, 239; ZamTGE, 90–93; Facs. KinkJD, Reprint supplement,45; Labanotation reconstruction: ThomMBT, 27, 34–38; harmonized version of music in MarrMBT, 41–42.

50b.   INGRATA

Choreography: Ascribed to Domenico da Piacenza by Guglielmo Ebreo.
Dance type: *Ballo,* 2 M and 1 W.
Source: *SBC, L. V. 29;* f. 70r,70v.
Music: Not preserved.
Edition: None.

51a.   JUPITER (also GIOVE, JOVE)

Choreography: Domenico da Piacenza.
Dance type: *Ballo,* 2 M and 1 W.
Sources:
1. *PBN, 972;* f. 17v,18r,18v.
2. *PBN, 973;* f. 35r,35v,36r.
3. *RBV, C 203;* f. 15r,15v,16r.
4. *FBNC, XIX 88;* f. 31v,32r,32v.
5. *SBC, L. V. 29;* f. 68v,69r,69v,70r. ⎤
6. *MBE, Ital. 82, a.J.9.4;* f. 25r,25v. ⎦ 3 dancers, not 4 as indicated in MSS.
7. *PBN, 476;* f. 47r,47v,48r.
8. *FML, A 13;* f. 45v,46r,46v.
9. *NYPL, 72–254;* f. 24r,24v.
Music:
1. *PBN, 972;* f. 17r,17v.
2. *PBN, 973;* f. 47r,47v.
3. *RBV, C 203;* f. 14v, 15r.
4. *PBN, 476;* f. 64r.
Remarks: Guglielmo chose GIOVE (= JOVE, genitive of JUPITER), retained his master's framework and created his own versions. *PBN 973, 476, FBNC* and *FML* are in agreement with one another; *SBC* and *MBE* agree with each other, but differ slightly from the others; *NYPL* has minor changes not

found in the others while Cornazano's seems somewhat related to Domenico's but abridged. The choreography with the music transcribed into modern notation and the given steps placed below the music is found in GomDMM, 304. This *ballo* is mentioned in TorresSQ, 192.

Editions: BianchiMD, 294–296; BianchiT, 137–139; HughesIM, 107–109; MazziCOR, 18; RonDVD, 40; ZamTGE, 82–84; KinkJD, Reprint supplement, 46.

52.   LAURO (also LAUGHRO, ZAURO)

Choreography: Lorenzo di Piero di Cosimo de' Medici.
Dance type: *Bassadanza,* 1 M and 1 W.
Sources:
1. *FBNC, XIX 88;* f. 27r,27v.
2. *FML, A 13;* f. 27r,27v.
3. *NYPL, 72–254;* f. 14v,15r.
Music: Not preserved.
Remarks: *FBNC* and *FML* are in agreement with each other. Despite a few initial changes, *NYPL* is similar to *FBNC* and *FML*. It is listed in *SBC* table of contents, but no choreography is given. It was performed in Florence's *piazza Santa Croce* to celebrate the presence of Pope Pius II in that city. (See RossUB, 16.)
Editions: ZamTGE, 68–69, here spelled ZAURO; choreography reconstructed in Labanotation by Ingrid Brainard and arranged to be danced to the music of *Casulle la nouvele,* BrainTCD, 4–13.

53.   LEGIADRA (also LEZADRA and LIZADRA)

Choreography: Guglielmo Ebreo da Pesaro.
Dance type: *Ballo,* 2 M and 2 W in couples.
Sources:
1. *PBN, 973;* f. 33r,33v,34r.
2. *FBNC, XIX 88;* f. 30r,30v.
3. *SBC, L.V. 29;* f. 82r,82v,83r,83v.
4. *PBN, 476;* f. 45r,45v,46r.
5. *FML, A 13;* f. 44r,44v.
6. *NYPL, 72–254;* f. 18v,19r.

Music:
1. *PBN, 973;* f. 51r,51v.
2. *PBN, 476;* f. 65r.
Remarks: All MSS in agreement with one another. Giovanni Ambrogio is given as the choreographer in *NYPL*. The *ballo* is mentioned in TorreSQ, 90.
Editions: HughesIM, 118–122; ZamTGE, 76–78; Facs. KinkJD, Reprint supplement, 46.

54a.   LEONZELLO (also LIONZELLO and LEONCELLO) *vecchio* (old)
Choreography: Domenico da Piacenza.
Dance type: *Ballo,* 1 M and 1 W.
Source: *PBN, 972;* f. 9r.
Music: *PBN, 972;* f. 8v,9r.
Remarks: The *ballo* is mentioned in TorreSQ, 35,36 and 81; in RossUB, 16; in VitPGG, 199; Labanotation reconstruction in ThomMBT, 31–33; harmonized version of music in MarrMBT, 40.
Edition: BianchiT, 124–125.

54b.   LEONCELLO
Choreography: Ascribed to Domenico da Piacenza by Guglielmo Ebreo.
Dance type: *Ballo,* 1 M and 1 W.
Sources:
1. *PBN, 973;* f. 40v,41r.
2. *FBNC, XIX 88;* f. 39r,39v.
3. *SBC, L.V. 29;* f. 63r,63v.
4. *PBN, 476;* f. 53v,54r.
5. *FML, A 13;* f. 53r.
6. *NYPL, 72–254;* f. 22r.
Music:
1. *PBN, 973;* f. 47r.
2. *RBV, C 203;* f. 20r.
3. *PBN, 476;* f. 63v.
Remarks: The *NYPL* entry on f. 22r is lacking in GalloBL, 76.
Editions: HughesIM, 115–118; ZamTGE, 103–104; Facs. KinkJD, Reprint supplement, 45.

54c. LIONCELLO
Choreography: Ascribed to Domenico da Piacenza by Guglielmo Ebreo.
Dance type: *Ballo,* 2 M and 1 W.
Sources:
1. *SBC, L.V. 29;* f. 79r,79v,80r.
2. *MBE, Ital. 82, a.J.9.4;* f. 27r,27v.
Music: Perhaps danced to music in *973.*
Edition: RonDVD, 43.

54d. LIONZELLO, *nuovo*
Choreography: Domenico da Piacenza.
Dance type: *Ballo,* 2 M and 1 W.
Source: *PBN, 972;* f. 9v,10r.
Music: Danced to LIONZELLO *vecchio.*
Edition: BianchiT, 125–126.

54e. LEONCELLO, *nuovo*
Choreography: Antonio Cornazano.
Dance type: *Ballo,* 2 M and 1 W.
Source: *RBV, C 203;* f. 20v,21r,21v,22r.
Music: *RBV, C 203;* f. 20r,20v.
Edition: MazziCOR, 21–22.

54f. LIONCELO
Choreography: Giovanni Ambrogio.
Dance type: *Balletto,* 2 M and 1 W.
Source: *NYPL, 72–254;* f. 30r,30v.
Music: Not preserved.
Edition: None.

55. LIPITIER
Choreography: Guglielmo Ebreo da Pesaro.
Dance type: *Ballo,* 2 M and 1 W.

Source: *FML, A 13;* f. 55v,56r.
Music: Not preserved.
Edition: PesSRT, 53–54.

56.   MALGRATIOSA

Choreography: Ascribed to Domenico da Piacenza by Guglielmo Ebreo.
Dance type: *Balletto,* 1 M and 1 W.
Source: *SBC, L.V. 29;* f. 73r,73v.
Music: Not preserved.
Edition: MazziUSC, 204.

57.   MALUM

Choreography: Guglielmo Ebreo da Pesaro.
Dance type: *Bassadanza,* 1 M and 1 W.
Source: *FBJ, D.I. 42;* f. 1v.
Music: Not preserved.
Edition: PuliOB, 14.

58.   MARCHEXANA (also MARCHESANA)

Choreography: Domenico da Piacenza.
Dance type: *Ballo,* 1 M and 1 W.
Sources:
1. *PBN, 972;* f. 16v,17r.
2. *PBN, 973;* f. 36v,37r,37v.
3. *FBNC, XIX 88;* f. 33v,34r.
4. *SBC, L.V. 29;* f. 63v,64r,64v.
5. *PBN, 476;* f. 49r,49v,50r.
6. *FML, A 13;* f. 47v,48r.
7. *NYPL, 72–254;* f. 23v.
Music:
1. *PBN, 972;* f. 16v.
2. *PBN, 973;* f. 49v,50r.
3. *PBN, 476;* f. 62r.
Remarks: Guglielmo retained the title and framework of Domenico's *ballo,*

but reworked it with slight changes. All of Guglielmo's MSS are in substantial agreement with one another.

Editions: BianchiT, 136–137; BianchiMD, 298–299; HughesIM, 123–126; ZamTGE, 87–88.

59.   MASTRI DI T[R]O[N]BONI

Choreography: Guglielmo Ebreo da Pesaro.
Dance type: *Ballo,* 2 M and 1 W.
Source: *FML, A 13;* f. 57r,57v,58r.
Music: Not preserved.
Remarks: The added letters in the title are taken from a passage in the choreography which calls for a "ripresa cola volta de' tronboni," an execution which occurs thrice during the *ballo.* The meaning is unknown to this writer.
Edition: PesSRT, 55.

60a.   MERCANTIA

Choreography: Domenico da Piacenza.
Dance type: *Ballo,* 3 M and 1 W.
Source: *PBN, 972;* f. 21r,21v,22r.
Music: *PBN, 972,* f. 21r.
Edition: BianchiT, 141–142; BrainCH, 355–356.

60b.   MERCANTIA

Choreography: Antonio Cornazano.
Dance type: *Ballo,* 3 M and 1 W.
Source: *RBV, C 203;* f. 13r,13v,14r,14v.
Music: *RBV, C 203,* f. 13v,14r.
Edition: MazziCOR, 16–18.

60c.   MERCANTIA (also MARCANCIA, MERCHANTIA, MERCANZIA, MARCANZZIA)

Choreography: Ascribed to Domenico da Piacenza by Guglielmo Ebreo.
Dance type: *Ballo,* 3 M and 1 W.

Sources:
1. *PBN, 973;* f. 41r,41v,42r.
2. *FBNC, XIX 88;* f. 39v,40r.
3. *PBN, 476;* f. 54v,55r.
4. *FML, A 13;* f. 53v,54r.
5. *NYPL, 72–254;* f. 21v,22r.
Music:
1. *PBN, 973;* f. 49r,49v.
2. *PBN, 476;* f. 64v.
Editions: BrainCH, 353–357; HughesIM, 126–129; ZamTGE, 105–107.

60d.   MERCHANTIA
Choreography: Ascribed to Domenico da Piacenza by Guglielmo Ebreo.
Dance type: *Ballo,* 3 M and 1 W.
Source: *SBC, L. V. 29;* f. 86r,86v,87r.
Music: Perhaps danced to *972,* f. 21r.
Remarks: This *ballo* is mentioned in TorreSQ, 89.
Edition: None.

61.   MESCHINA
Choreography: Ascribed to Domenico da Piacenza by Guglielmo Ebreo.
Dance type: *Bassadanza,* 2 M and 1 W.
Source: *SBC, L. V. 29;* f. 51v,52r.
Music: Not preserved.
Edition: MazziUSC, 199.

62a.   MIGNOTTA, *vecchia*
Choreography: Domenico da Piacenza.
Dance type: *Bassadanza,* any number of dancers *à la fila*.
Source: *PBN, 972;* f. 26v,27r.
Music: Not preserved.
Editions: BianchiT, 148–149; Labanotation reconstruction in ThomMBT, 29–33; arranged to be danced to a harmonized version of the *bassadanza* tenor, *Cançon de' pifari* (p. 57) in MarrMBT, 39.

62b.   MIGNOTTA, *nuova*
Choreography: Domenico da Piacenza.
Dance type: *Bassadanza;* any number of dancers *à la fila.*
Source: *PBN, 972;* f. 27r,27v.
Music: Not preserved.
Edition: BianchiT, 149–150.

62c.   MIGNOTTA, *nuova.*
Choreography: Antonio Cornazano.
Dance type: *Bassadanza;* 1 M and 1 W *à la fila.*
Source: *RBV, C 203;* f. 29r,29v.
Music: Not preserved.
Remarks: Cornazano borrowed the opening steps from Domenico's treatise, but continued with his own creation. He suggests that as many dancers take part in the dance as the room is spacious enough to accommodate them. The *bassadanza* is mentioned in TorreSQ, 91.
Editions: BianchiMD, 293–294; BianchiT, 148–149; MazziCOR, 26–27; RonDVD, 34–35; ZamTGE, 44–45; ZanAC, 290: choreography reconstructed in ThomMBT, 29–30.

62d.   MIGNOTTA (also MIGNOTA, MIGNIOTTA, MINGNIOTTA)
Choreography: Ascribed to Domenico da Piacenza by Guglielmo Ebreo.
Dance type: *Bassadanza, à la fila,* no number specified.
Sources:
1. *PBN, 973;* f. 24v,25r.
2. *FBNC, XIX 88;* f. 18v,19r.
3. *SBC, L.V. 29;* f. 45r,45v,46r.
4. *MBE, Ital. 82, a.J.9.4;* f. 21r,21v.
5. *PBN, 476;* f. 35v,36r.
6. *FML, A 13;* f. 19v.
Music: Not preserved.
Editions: BianchiMD, 293–294; RonDVD, 34–35; ZamTGE, 44–45.

62e.   MINGNIOTTA
Choreography: Ascribed to Domenico da Piacenza by Guglielmo Ebreo.
Dance type: *Bassadanza,* 1 M and 1 W.
Source: *NYPL, 72–254;* f. 9v.
Music: Not preserved.
Remarks: Guglielmo accepted Domenico's initial steps, then continued with a new choreography. All of his MSS are in substantial agreement with one another, although with such minor changes as substituting *continenze* for *riverenze. NYPL* is a different version, but retains the framework.
Edition: None.

63.   MIGNOTA
Choreography: Ascribed to Domenico da Piacenza by Guglielmo Ebreo.
Dance type: *Bassadanza,* 3 dancers.
Source: *SBC, L.V. 29;* f. 41r.
Music: Not preserved.
Edition: MazziUSC, 196.

64.   MODERNA
Choreography: Ascribed to Domenico da Piacenza by Guglielmo Ebreo.
Dance type: *Bassadanza,* 2 dancers.
Source: *SBC, L.V. 29;* f. 37v,38r.
Music: Not preserved.
Edition: MassiUSC, 194.

65.   MOROSA
Choreography: Ascribed to Domenico da Piacenza by Guglielmo Ebreo.
Dance type: *Bassadanza,* 1 M and 1 W.
Source: *SBC, L.V. 29;* f. 42r,42v.
Music: Not preserved.
Edition: MazziUSC, 196.

66.   MOZA DI BISCAIE
Choreography: Guglielmo Ebreo da Pesaro.
Dance type: *Ballo,* 2 M and 1 W.
Source: *FML, A 13;* f. 54v,55r,55v.
Music: Not preserved.
Remarks: The music of this *ballo* may have been identical to the French *chanson, Une Musque de Buscaya (PBN,* coll. Rothschild, VI–3 bis–66), though a comparison of the choreographies shows different dances. (See LesDCD, 177, No. 22.) Josquin des Prez based his *Missa Una Musque de Buscaya* on this tune. (See JosqWW, x–xii and 5–6.) The *ballo* is mentioned in TorreSQ, 215n and in CatCCM, 200.
Edition: PesSRT, 52–53.

67.   NOBILE
Choreography: Ascribed to Domenico da Piacenza by Guglielmo Ebreo.
Dance type: *Bassadanza,* 3 dancers *à la fila.*
Source: *SBC, L.V. 29;* f. 37v.
Music: Not preserved.
Edition: MazziUSC, 194.

68.   PARTITA CRUDELE
Choreography: Domenico da Piacenza?
Dance type: *Bassadanza,* 1 M and 1 W.
Sources:
1. *FBNC, XIX 88;* f. 25r,25v,26r.
2. *SBC, L.V. 29;* f. 59r,59v.
3. *FML, A 13;* f. 25v,26r.
4. *NYPL, 72–254;* f. 12r.
Music: Not preserved.
Remarks: *SBC* ascribes its choreography to Domenico, which may perhaps explain the fact that the *SBC* choreography differs considerably from *FBNC, FML* and *NYPL* that ascribe the choreography to Giuseppe Ebreo. This *bassadanza* is mentioned in TorreSQ, 91.
Edition: ZamTGE, 63–65.

69.   PATIENTIA (also PAZIENZA)

Choreography: Guglielmo Ebreo da Pesaro.
Dance type: *Bassadanza,* 2 M and 2 W.
Sources:
1. *PBN, 973;* f. 29r,29v,30r.
2. *FBNC, XIX 88;* f. 23r,23v,24r.
3. *SBC, L.V. 29;* f. 56r,56v,57r,57v.
4. *PBN, 476;* f. 40v,41r,41v.
5. *FML, A 13;* f. 23v,24r.
6. *NYPL, 72–254;* f. 10r.
Music: Not preserved.
Remarks: All MSS in substantial agreement with one another save *SBC,* which opens differently, then continues with the choreography of the other MSS, not, however, without a few minor changes. This *bassadanza* is mentioned in TorreSQ, 91.
Edition: ZamTGE, 57–59.

70.   PELLEGRINA (also PELYGRYNA, PEREGRINA, PELEGRINA)

Choreography: Guglielmo Ebreo da Pesaro.
Dance type: *Bassadanza,* 1 M and 1 W.
Sources:
1. *FBJ, D.I. 42;* f. 1r.
2. *PBN, 973;* f. 26v,27r.
3. *FBNC, XIX 88;* f. 20r,20v.
4. *SBC, L.V. 29;* f. 46r,46v.
5. *PBN, 476;* f. 37v,38r.
6. *FML, A 13;* f. 20v,21r,21v.
7. *NYPL, 72–254;* f. 10v,11r.
Music: Not preserved.
Remarks: *PBN 973, 476, FBNC* and *FML* are in agreement with one another. *SBC* is substantially the same; the first choreography in *FBJ* contains *salti,* which were dropped in later sources. It was performed in Florence's *piazza Santa Croce* to celebrate the presence of Pope Pius II in that city. (See RossUB, 16).
Editions: PuliOB, 13; ZamTGE, 48–50.

71. PETIT RIENSE (also PETIT VRIENS)
Choreography: Giovanni Ambrogio.
Dance type: *Ballo Francese,* 3 dancers.
Source: *PBN, 476;* f. 59r,59v.
Music: *PBN, 476;* f. 65v.
Edition: HughesIM, 129–130.

72. PETIT ROSE
Choreography: Ascribed to Domenico da Piacenza by Guglielmo Ebreo.
Dance type: *Ballo,* 1 M and 1 W.
Sources:
1. *PBN, 973;* f. 34v,35r.
2. *FBNC, XIX 88;* f. 31v.
3. *SBC, L.V. 29;* f. 84v,85r.
4. *PBN, 47b;* f. 47r.
5. *FML, A 13;* f. 45v. (Here spelled, PRESZIOSO, but choreography same as PETIT ROSE.)
6. *NYPL, 72–254;* f. 20r.
Music: Not preserved.
Remarks: All MSS in substantial agreement with one another, save *SBC,* which opens with 12 tempi of *piva* in lieu of 16.
Edition: ZamTGE, 81–82, here spelled PETTIROSE.

73. PIATOSA (also PIETOSA)
Choreography: Guglielmo Ebreo da Pesaro.
Dance type: *Bassadanza:* 1 M and 1 W.
Sources:
1. *PBN, 973;* f. 25r,25v.
2. *FBNC, XIX 88;* f. 19r,19v.
3. *SBC, L.V. 29;* f. 50v,51r,51v.
4. *PBN, 476;* f. 36r,36v.
5. *FML, A 13;* f. 19v,20r.
6. *NYPL, 72–254;* f. 10v.
Music: Not preserved.

Remarks: All MSS in substantial agreement. *SBC* introduces 2 *continenze* first, then proceeds with the same choreography as the other MSS.
Editions: ZamTGE, 45–46; choreography translated into English in KinkJD, Reprint supplement, 19.

74.   PIZOCHARA (also PINZOCHERA)

Choreography: Domenico da Piacenza.
Dance type: *Ballo,* 4 M and 4 W.
Sources:
1. *PBN, 972;* f. 12r,12v.
2. *SBC, L.V. 29;* f. 71r,71v.
Music:
1. *PBN, 972;* f. 12r.
2. *PBN, 973;* f. 48r,48v.
3. *PBN, 476;* f. 63r.
Remarks: Guglielmo retained Domenico's framework, and there are, indeed, sections quite similar, but some directions have been expunged. The *ballo* is mentioned in TorreSQ, 91 and 192.
Editions: BianchiT, 128–129; HughesIM, 131–133; MazziUSC, 203.

75a.   PREXONERA

Choreography: Domenico da Piacenza.
Dance type: *Ballo,* 1 M and 1 W.
Source: *PBN, 972;* f. 14v,15r.
Music: *PBN, 972;* f. 14v.
Editions: BianchiMD, 296–298; BianchiT, 133–134; HughesIM, 134–136.

75b.   PRESONIERA (also PRIGIONERA, PRESONERA)

Choreography: Ascribed to Domenico da Piacenza by Guglielmo Ebreo.
Dance type: *Ballo,* 1 M and 1 W.

Sources:
1. *PBN, 973;* f. 36r,36v.
2. *FBNC, XIX 88;* f. 32v,33r,33v.
3. *SBC, L.V. 29;* f. 67v,68r,68v.
4. *PBN, 476;* f. 48r,48v,49r.
5. *FML, A 13;* f. 46r,47r,47v.
6. *NYPL, 72–254;* f. 23v,24r.

Music:
1. *PBN, 973;* f. 46r.
2. *PBN, 476;* f. 62v.

Remarks: Guglielmo's choreography does not resemble Domenico's. His six MSS are substantially in agreement with one another. *PBN 476* is a copy of *973* as *FML* is of *FBNC*. *SBC* contains minor changes, while *NYPL* replaces some sections with other material. The *ballo* is mentioned in TorreSQ, 91 and 192.

Editions: HughesIM, 134–136; ZamTGE, 84–86.

76. PRINCIPESSA

Choreography: Guglielmo Ebreo da Pesaro.
Dance type: *Bassadanza,* any number of dancers *à la fila.*
Sources:
1. *PBN, 973;* f. 30v,31r.
2. *FBNC, XIX 88;* f. 24v,25r.
3. *SBC, L.V. 29;* f. 47r,47v,48r.
4. *MBE, Ital. 82, a.J.9.4;* f. 21v,22r.
5. *PBN, 476;* f. 42r,42v.
6. *FML, A 13;* f. 24v,25r,25v.
7. *NYPL, 72–254;* f. 11v,12r.

Music: Not preserved.

Remarks: All but two of Guglielmo's MSS are in substantial agreement with one another save for an occasional substitution of a *continenza* for a *riverenza.* *SBC* and *MBE* differ from the others in that some sections have been replaced with new material.

Editions: RonDVD, 35; ZamTGE, 60–62.

77.   PRINCIPESSA
Choreography: Guglielmo Ebreo da Pesaro.
Dance type: *Ballo,* 3 dancers.
Source: *SBC, L.V. 29;* f. 87v,88r.
Music: Not preserved.
Edition: MazziUSC, 208.

78.   RAIA
Choreography: Ascribed to Domenico da Piacenza by Guglielmo Ebreo.
Dance type: *Balletto,* 1 M and 1 W or 2 M and 1 W.
Source: *SBC, L.V. 29;* f. 72v,73r.
Music: Not preserved.
Edition: MazziUSC, 204.

79a.   REALE
Choreography: Ascribed to Domenico da Piacenza by Guglielmo Ebreo.
Dance type: *Bassadanza,* 1 M and 1 W.
Sources:
1. *FBJ, D.I. 42;* f. 4r.
2. *PBN, 973;* f. 23r.
3. *FBNC, XIX 88;* f. 17r.
4. *PBN, 476;* f. 33v.
5. *FML, A 13;* f. 17v,18r.
6. *NYPL, 72–254;* f. 12v.
Music: Not preserved.
Editions: PuliOB, 19; ZamTGE, 38–39.

79b.   REALE
Choreography: Entered under *Rubric* as the creation of Domenico da Piacenza, but unascribed in the choreography.
Dance type: *Bassadanza,* 2 dancers.
Source: *SBC, L.V. 29;* f. 36r,36v.
Music: Not preserved.

Remarks: *PBN 973* and *476* are in agreement with each other; *FBNC, FML* and *NYPL* agree with the above save for the last two lines which call for 4 *continenze* in lieu of 1 *riverenza. FBJ* has sections expunged in later MSS, while *SBC* is a different choreography.
Edition: None.

80.   RE DI SPAGNA (see music, page 72)
Remarks: No choreography preserved, but see No. 8 LA BASSA DI CASTIGLIA and No. 86 LA SPAGNA.

81.   ROSSINA
Choreography: Presumably by Guglielmo/Giovanni.
Dance type: *Balletto,* 2 M and 1 W.
Source: *NYPL, 72–254;* f. 26v,27r.
Music: Not preserved.
Remarks: See VOLTATE IN ÇA ROSINA. ROSSINA is mentioned in RossLAC, 413, 414n and 420n.
Edition: None.

82a.   ROSTIBOLI GIOIOSO (also GIOIOSO)
Choreography: Ascribed to Domenico da Piacenza by Guglielmo Ebreo.
Dance type: *Ballo,* 1 M and 1 W.
Sources:
1. *PBN, 973;* f. 32r,32v.
2. *FBNC, XIX 88;* f. 28v,29r.
3. *SBC, L.V. 29;* f. 62r,62v.
4. *PBN, 476;* f. 44r,44v.
5. *FML, A 13;* f. 42v,43r. (Entered erroneously as GOVE.)
6. *NYPL, 72–254;* f. 25r.
Music: *PBN, 476;* f. 66r.
Editions: BrainCH, 321–334; CranMFS, 85, 97–101; HughesIM, 102–106; JackFCB, English translation of choreography, 38, music 31 and 39; MazziUSC, 201; MeyEMBD, 21; RonDVD, 42; SmithFCD, 106–107; ZamTGE, 72–74.

82b.   GIOIOSO (= ROSTIBOLI GIOIOSO)
Choreography: Ascribed to Domenico da Piacenza by Guglielmo Ebrco in *SBC* rubric, but unascribed in choreography.
Dance type: *Ballo,* 2 M and 1 W.
Sources:
1. *SBC, L. V. 29;* f. 77v,78r,78v,79r.
2. *MBE, Ital. 82, a.J.9.4;* f. 26r,26v,27r.
3. *NYPL, 72–254;* f. 25v,26r,26v (*Balletto*).
Music: Not preserved.
Remarks: The music, transcribed into modern notation with the steps added below, is found in HeartzFCB, 364. See ToulABD, No. 20, where it is a *bassedanse.* See also ClosMBD, No. 55. The *ballo* is mentioned in TorreSQ, 35–36 and 81; in RossLAC, 232, 293 and 419; in RossUB, 16; and in VitPGG, 199.
Edition: None. MazziUSC, 206, states that the choreography has been edited by ZamTGE, 72–74, but the reference is to No. 82a *supra.*

83.   SANZOMEZA (or GIANZONETTA)
Choreography: Presumably by Guglielmo / Giovanni.
Dance type: *Ballo,* 2 M and 1 W.
Source: *NYPL, 72–254;* f. 36r,36v.
Music: Not preserved.
Edition: None

84.   SE NON DORMI DONNA ALSCIOLTTA
Choreography: Guglielmo Ebreo da Pesaro.
Dance type: *Ballo,* 2 M and 1 W.
Source: *FML, A 13;* f. 56v,57r.
Music: Not preserved.
Remarks: It was a *canzona.* A *frottola* titled, "SE NON DORMI, ASCOLTA" is included in Ottaviano Petrucci's *Frottole libro terzo,* 53v,54r. (See JeppFROT, 17–18.) LA FIA GUILMIN, No. 33 and VOLTATE IN ÇA ROSINA, No. 92 are two instances where the tenors of the *frottole* correspond to the dance tunes.
Edition: PesSRT, 54–55.

85. SOBRIA
Choreography: Domenico da Piacenza.
Dance type: *Ballo,* 5 M and 1 W.
Sources:
1. *PBN, 972;* f. 22v,23r,23v.
2. *RBV, C 203;* f. 27r,27v,28r,28v.
Music:
1. *PBN, 972;* f. 22r,22v.
2. *RBV, C 203;* f. 25v,26r,26v.
Remarks: Antonio borrowed the theme of pursuit (one woman as the quarry) from Domenico. Several sections correspond to each other in substance, in others new sections are introduced. The *Ballo* is mentioned in TorreSQ, 81 and 196.
Editions: BianchiT, 142–145; BrainCH, 358–366; HughesIM, 137–141; MazziCOR, 24–25; ZanAC, 289–290.

86. SPAGNA, LA (also RE DI SPAGNA, but compare with LA BASSA DI CASTIGLIA)
Choreography: Ascribed to Domenico da Piacenza by Guglielmo Ebreo.
Dance type: *Bassadanza,* 2 dancers.
Sources:
1. *SBC, L.V. 29;* f. 36v.
2. *NYPL, 72–254;* f. 36r.
Music: Perhaps danced to the music of RE DI SPAGNA.
Remarks: Both MSS in complete agreement with each other. An English translation of this *bassadanza* (*SBC*) is found in DolDSI, 18–24, including a harmonized version of the *bassadanza* tenor, RE DI SPAGNA in *RBV*. See No. 80. This dance is mentioned in RossLAC, 416. See also GomCVC, xli–xliii; HeartzHBD, 18–19; MeyEMBD, *passim.*
Edition: MazziUSC, 194.

87. SPERO
Choreography: Guglielmo Ebreo da Pesaro.
Dance type: *Ballo,* 1 M and 2 W.

Sources:
1. *PBN, 973;* f. 42v,43r,43v.
2. *FBNC, XIX 88;* f. 38r,38v.
3. *PBN, 476;* f. 56r,56v,57r.
4. *FML, A 13;* f. 52r,52v,53r.
5. *NYPL, 72–254;* f. 21r,21v.

Music:
1. *PBN, 973;* f. 50r.
2. *PBN, 476;* f. 62r.

Remarks: All MSS are in agreement with one another. Guglielmo ascribed the *ballo* to Domenico in *FBNC, FML* and *NYPL*. In *PBN 973* the *ballo* names Guglielmo as the choreographer, while Giovanni Ambrogio is given in *PBN 476*.

Editions: HughesIM, 141–144; ZamTGE, 100–102.

88.   **TESARA**

Choreography: Domenico da Piacenza.
Dance type: *Ballo,* 6 M and 4 W.
Source: *PBN, 972;* f. 24r,24v,25r,25v,26r.
Music: *PBN, 972;* f. 23v,24r.
Remarks: Mentioned in TorreSQ, 192.
Editions: BianchiT, 145–148; BrainCH, 347–352; HughesIM, 144–147.

89.   **VENUS**

Choreography: Lorenzo di Piero di Cosimo de' Medici.
Dance type: *Bassadanza,* 2 M and 1 W.
Sources:
1. *FBNC, XIX 88;* f. 26r,26v,27r.
2. *FML, A 13;* f. 26r,26v,27r.
3. *NYPL, 72–254;* f. 14r,14v.

Music: Not preserved.

Remarks: All MSS in complete agreement with one another. This *bassadanza* is listed in the table of contents in *SBC,* but it was not choreographed. An English translation of the choreography is found in DolDSI, 25–33, including a harmonized version of a French *chanson* titled, *Venus, tu ma pris.*

Edition: ZamTGE, 65–68.

90. VERÇEPPE

Choreography: Domenico da Piacenza.
Dance type: *Ballo,* 3 M and 2 W.
Sources:
1. *PBN, 972;* f. 13r,13v,14r,14v.
2. *RBV, C 203;* f. 17r,17v,18r.
Music:
1. *PBN, 972;* f. 13r.
2. *RBV, C 203;* f. 16r,16v,17r.
Remarks: Cornazano's choreography is an abridged version of Domenico's. This *ballo* is mentioned in TorreSQ, 81 and 192.
Editions: BianchiT, 130–131; HughesIM, 147–150; MazziCOR, 18–20; ZanAC, 288; music transcribed into modern notation in BrainTCD, 14, facs. viii; Labanotation reconstruction in BrainTCD, 15–23.

91. VITA DI CHOLINO, LA

Choreography: Presumably by Guglielmo/Giovanni.
Dance type: *Balletto,* 2 M and 1 W.
Source: *NYPL, 72–254;* f. 27v,28r.
Music: Not preserved, but see K. Jeppesen, "Venetian Folk-Songs of the Renaissance," *Papers of the American Musicological Society,* 1939, 69–71.
Remarks: The incipit of this *balletto* also exists as the title of a *frottola.* See JeppFROT, 63–64 and 107, and Pope-Kanazawa, *The Musical Manuscript Montecassino 871,* 534–535, and Appendix II by Ingrid Brainard.
Edition: None.

92. VOLTATE IN ÇA ROSINA

Choreography: Giovanni Ambrogio.
Dance type: *Ballo,* 1 M and 2 W.
Source: *PBN, 476;* f. 57r,57v,58r.
Music: *PBN, 476,* f. 64v.
Remarks: A *frottola* with the same incipit is found in JeppFROT, 35, its melody identical to the melody of this *ballo.* Real or fictitious, *Rosina* appears to have captured the imagination of several composers. The above is one of the many *frottole* and *villotte* containing the name *Rosina,* listed in TorreSQ, 81,

83–86, 88–90, 113, 123, 139, 142, 218, 236, 252, 311 and 328. Writing in 1540, Andrea Calmo includes it with two other dances as being of "nostri tempi passai" (our times passed). See RossLAC, 232. It first appeared in Giovanni Ambrogio's treatise (c. 1480) and provides evidence of the longevity of certain dances. For other early 16th century Italian and French sources where *Rosina, Lioncello, Gioioso [Rostiboli]* and *Anello* are mentioned, see HeartzFCB, 373–375.
Edition: HughesIM, 150–151.

93.   ZOGLIOXA
Choreography: Domenico da Piacenza.
Dance type: *Bassadanza,* no number of dancers given.
Source: *PBN, 972;* f. 28r.
Music: Not preserved.
Edition: BianchiT, 149.

Notes

1. Six of them are actually versions of Guglielmo's first treatise, *PBN 973* (see further). But there was another version of which only two folios have been recovered and are now preserved in a collection with other miscellaneous documents in Florence's Biblioteca Nazionale Centrale, *Palatino 1021* (see BrainRDM, 21–44). Written on paper (145 x 222 mm) in a cursive hand, crowded and almost illegible, the two folios begin with the last three lines of the introductory sonnet and continue through the *Prohemium* and the sections of *Misura, Memoria, Partire del terreno, Aiere* and end abruptly at the bottom of the page with the words, "in fine che'l tempo misurato," of the section on *Maniera*. Almost word for word *Palatino 1021* appears to be a copy of *FBNC*. There are three sets of folio numbers: the first on the upper right corner with the numbers crossed out—141 and 142; the second pair of numbers on the top margin—55 and 56; and the third more recent addition are those on the lower margin—155 and 156, which are numbers given to those pages when they were bound together with non-related documents.

2. Four other dance masters are named: Giulio in Bologna, Phylippo, Giuseppe Ebreo and Marjotto da Perugia, of whom nothing is known. (See Nos. 16b, 20, 39 and 68.)

3. MichEDM, 110.

4. HeartzFCB, 366.

5. Folio 2v.

6. Although Giovanni Ambrogio's mémoires in *PBN 476*, f. 65r–80v, make no mention of Florence, Eitner affirms that the *bassedanze Lauro* and *Venus*, with choreographies by Lorenzo de' Medici, establish proof of Guglielmo's presence in Florence as dancing master to the Medicean court (EitBQL, IV, 415).

7. Unfortunately, while Giovanni Ambrogio recalls parties, lavish entertainments, weddings and other public ceremonies, he fails to give the dates of those events which would have helped immeasurably in establishing the period of residence at the various courts. However, by examining documents of historical

importance such as princely nuptials and other civic affairs, Giovanni Roncaglia succeeded in placing Ambrogio in Ferrara at the wedding of the marquis Leonello and Maria d'Alfonso d'Aragona in 1444; in Camerino at the wedding of Alessandro Sforza and Costanza Varano in the same year; in Milan when duke Alessandro made his triumphant entry into that city in 1450 (RonDVD, 27); in Naples 1455–57*, Urbino 1460*, Forli 1462*, Urbino and Faenza in 1471*. (Those asterisked have been supplied to me through the kindness of Dr. Prof. Alberto Gallo of the University of Bologna.) Guglielmo/ Ambrogio must have been Domenico's contemporary because he declares in *PBN 476*, f. 29v, in *SBC*, f. 27v, and in *MBE*, f. 17r, that he had accumulated 30 years' experience in the science and art of the dance. He was still with the living and dancing in 1481 (see below). In the light of these events, Guglielmo/ Ambrogio was born between 1410 and 1415 and died sometime after 1481 (see also BrainRDM).

8. Thirty-four choreographies are attributed to Domenico by Guglielmo, but in many instances his choreographies differ considerably from his master's though the same title is shared.

9. The poem on f. 44r–45v of the Parisian codex *973* has been reproduced in KinkJD, 40–42.

10. Albano Sorbelli's *Inventario dei Manoscritti delle Biblioteche d'Italia*, Vol. 41, Florence, Olschki, 1930, 186, erroneously states that the recipients of the offering were the newlyweds, Buffetti–Berutti!

11. Although no abjuration of faith has been found, there is evidence which supports his having embraced Christianity, the first in a letter written by Guido da Bagno on 24 January 1481 pertinent to Isabella d'Este's skill as a dancer, who was then at the tender age of seven:

> La Ill … Isabella per due volte ballo anchor lei cum quello Ambroso, quale fu zudeo et sta col Illmo S. Duca de Urbino, che è suo maestro di ballar. (The illustrious … Isabella danced twice with that Ambroso, who was a Jew and is also the dancing master of the illustrious seignior, the duke of Urbino.) See A. Luzio, *I precettori d'Isabella d'Este*.   Ancona, 1887, 12.

A second letter by Giovanni Ambrogio to Ippolita Sforza from Naples expresses his satisfaction with the progress made by her daughters, Lionora and Beatrice, in their study of the dance and his desire to return to Milan, requesting her to intercede in his behalf. Of relevance is the word *Yhesus* on the letter head (see MotMCS, 61–62). Lastly, *NYPL* often carries the name of the choreographer, in this case "Giovanni Ambrogio, che fu ebreo" (who was Jewish). See *NYPL*, f. 19v, 22r, 22v, 26v and 30r. But the most convincing testimony is the similarity of *PBN 476* with the earlier *973*, such as the Socratic dialogue, the same choreographies and music, and the names of the rulers and their courts.

12. Toscanini's letter to Dr. Ingrid Brainard dated March 16, 1962, is deposited in the Dance Collection of the New York Public Library.

13. Etymologic dictionaries are of no assistance since most of these terms are a kind of dance jargon well known at that time, but perhaps considered unworthy of recording by encyclopedists. One can hazard a guess at their meanings, keeping in mind that the duration of such *movimenti accidentali* according to Domenico, do not exceed one quarter of a bar (*972*, f. 3r), but consult BrainTCD, iv; BrainBBB, 73–74; KinkJD, 13–14 and SachWHD, 306–310.

14. *PBN 972, 973, 476*, and *RBV 203*. There may be two other Italian *bassedanze* preserved in the *Schedelscher Liederbuch* (Munich, Stadtsbibliothek, *MS. 3232*, f. 131r). Only the melodies are given and notated in semibreves and breves. The rubric placed below the first line of music, *Carmina ytalica utilia pro coreis*, would appear to confirm both melodies as dances, though no choreographies are given. I am indebted to Dr. Raymond Meylan of Münchenstein, Switzerland, for this information (see MeyEMBD, 78–81). [That these tunes found their way into the repertoire of transalpine *basses danses* is attested by Manfred Bukofzer, who identified the first tune with *La franchoise* (ClosMBD, No. 7) in his "Changing Aspects of Medieval and Renaissance Music," *Musical Quarterly*, LXIV (1958), 15; and by Daniel Heartz who identified the second tune with *Le petit rouen* (HeartzBD, 306, fn.3).] Eileen Southern suggests the existence of yet another *bassadanza* used as the tenor for Faugues's *Missa bassedanse*, preserved in the *Denkmäler der Tonkunst in Oesterreich*, VII, 67 (SoutBDM, 740).

15. *PBN 476*, f. 32r.

16. The dance tunes transcribed into modern notation are also published in HughesIM.

17. Usually indicated in the music by symbols of the four prolations:

tempus perfectum minoris prolationis = ¾
tempus imperfectum maioris prolationis = ⁶⁄₈
tempus perfectum maioris prolationis = ⁹⁄₈
tempus imperfectum minoris prolationis = ²⁄₄

and in the choreography by such directions as found in *Le Geloxia (PBN 972)* "sei tempi di saltarello in misura quaternaria," (six tempi of *saltarello* in *quaternaria* measure), i.e. to dance the *saltarello* step unit, normally ⁹⁄₈, in *quaternaria*, normally in ²⁄₄.

18. Employing digital computers in his study of the armatures (frameworks) of *chansons* and *bassedanses*, Raymond Meylan has succeeded in demonstrating some startling relationships between songs and dances of the fifteenth century. (MeyRPBD).

Section B

the music transcribed into modern notation

Editorial Commentary: Music

The range of the dance tune is shown at the beginning of the composition by black notes without stems. The time signature in brackets reflects the meaning of the prolation symbol; if lacking, the particular grouping of the notes sufficed to identify the meter. Only the treble or bass clef has been employed. With the exceptions of AMOROSO and the three *bassedanze*, all melodies have been transposed one octave higher to keep them within the ambit of the staff. The application of complementary accidentals (*musica ficta*) was well known to all competent performers in the fifteenth century. We have no precise knowledge of these principles, but in this edition an editorial accidental is placed above the note (and not valid beyond that note), and is employed to avoid the tritone and augmented seconds in sequence. Bar lines, absent in the original, are regularly placed. In keeping with musicological practice, note values have been reduced; the brevis □   = a half note.

1. AMOROSO

Ballo Francese

PBN 476, f. 65v.

Giovanni Ambrogio

*The number followed by x indicates a three-fold repetition.
1) *Semibrevis* in MS.   2) and 3) are *Minimae* in MS.

2. ANELLO

Ballo

PBN 972, f. 16r.

Domenico da Piacenza

1) *Minima* in MS.   2) *Longa* in MS.

3. BEL FIORE

Ballo

PBN 972, f. 15r.   Domenico da Piacenza

1) F clef in MS.
2) Superfluous *minim* rest omitted in transcription.
3) *Longa* in MS.

4. BEL REGUARDO

Ballo

PBN 972, f. 7v.   Domenico da Piacenza

1) F clef sign in MS scribal error.   2) No flat signature in *RBV 203*.
3) Pitched a fifth lower in *PBN 973* and *476*.

5. CANÇON DE'PIFARI DICTO EL FERRARESE

Tenore da Bassadanza

PBV, C 203; f. 32v-33r.

Antonio Cornazano

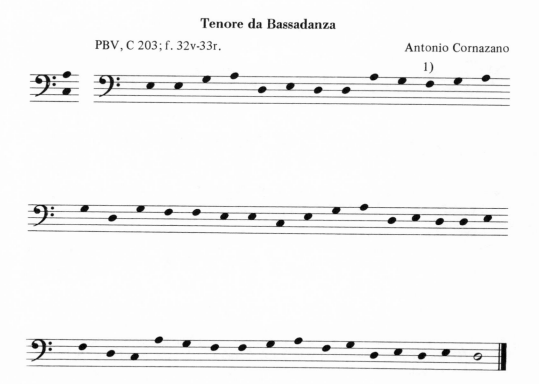

Choreography: Not preserved.   1) Superfluous flat omitted on F.

Remarks: No mensuration sign in MS. Mentioned in TorreSQ, 214.

Editions: Hughes IM, 152; JackFCB (music), 37; CranMSF, 98 and 103-104; MeyEMBD, 12.

6. COLLINETTO

Tenore da Bassadanza

RBV, C 203; f. 33r-33v.   Antonio Cornazano

Choreography: Not preserved.

Remarks: No mensuration sign given. The melody of this *bassadanza* bears a strong re-
semblance to the French *chanson, Biance flour* employed as the tenor of a
keyboard piece in the codex *Faenza 117*. (See PlamKM, No. 24 and a comparison of both melodies in MarrDBD). Cornazano's *bassadanza* tenor can be found
in WallBO, Nos. 56 and 57, as a *cantus firmus* in 2 three-part settings. At times
the melody is fragmented, absent for a measure or two, and at other times it is
skillfully hidden with coloration. Here the composition is titled *Collinit*. (See
SouthSKBD, 116-117.

Editions: Hughes IM, 152; CranMFS, 98 and 104; JackFCB, 37; MeyEMBD, 12;
MarrDBD, 138-139.

7. COLONNESE

Ballo

PBN 973, f. 50v-51r.   Guglielmo Ebreo da Pesaro

1) *Minim* in *PBN 973*; *Semibrevis* in *476*.
2) Scribal error; it is clearly *tempus perfectum minoris prolationis*.
3) Reading from *476*.

8. LA FIA GUILMIN

Ballo

PBN 972, f. 18v-19r.

Domenico da Piacenza

1) I am indebted to Ingrid Brainard who has pointed out that F clef in both the Domenico and Cornazano (*RBV*) MSS, was erroneously placed on the third line rather than on the fourth. (See Pope-Kanazawa, *The Musical Manuscript Montecassino 871*, pp. 531-533). I have arbitrarily raised the melody one octave in view of the 1) unusually low register, 2) consensus that improvised harmonies were added below the melody. Bars 29, 30, the first half of 31 and 38 omitted in *RBV*.

2) *Semibrevis* in MS.

3) B flat in *RBV*.

4) *Longa* in MS.

9. LA GILOXIA
Ballo

PBN 972, f. 11r.

Domenico da Piacenza

1) Flat before F.

10. GRATIOSO
Ballo

PBN 973, f. 50v.

Guglielmo Ebreo da Pesaro

1) F in MS.
2) *PBN 476* reads

3) *Semiminima* in MS.   4) *Minima* in MS.

11. INGRATA

Ballo

1) ℭ in *PBN 973* and *476*.

12. JUPITER

Ballo

PBN 972, f. 17r-17v.   Domenico da Piacenza

1) No mensuration sign in *RBV*.

2) The mensuration sign is misleading. Domenico writes that the dancers perform three tempi of saltarelli in *mexura quaternaria*.

3) The mensuration sign for *tempus perfectum maioris prolationis* must be a scribal error.

13. LEGIADRA

Ballo

PBN 973, f. 51r-51v.

Guglielmo Ebreo da Pesaro

1) Superfluous C *semibrevis* omitted.
2) Superfluous C *semibrevis* omitted.
3) *Semibrevis* in MS.

14. LEONZELLO

Ballo

PBN 972, f. 8v-9r.

Domenico da Piacenza

1) No flat in *RBV 203*.
2) *Pausa minima* in MS.
In lieu of 5 repetitions of section 1, *PBN 476* interpolates a slight melodic variation
for the 4th and 5th repetition as follows:

15. MARCHEXANA

Ballo

PBN 972, f. 16v.   Domenico da Piacenza

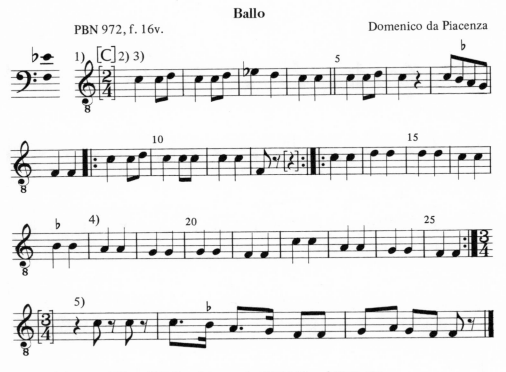

1) No clef sign in MS.   2) B flat signature in *PBN 973* and *PBN 476*.
3) Three initial *pause minimae* omitted in transcription.
4) Sharp before A omitted.   5) Two initial *pause minimae*.
   From bar 26 *PBN 476* reads:

16. MERCANTIA

Ballo

PBN 972, f. 21r.   Domenico da Piacenza

1) No mensuration sign given in *PBN 973* and *PBN 476*.

17. PETIT RIENSE

Ballo Francese

1) *Minima* in MS.
2) *Minima* in MS.
3) *Minima* in MS.

18. PIZOCHARA

Ballo

PBN 972, f. 12r.   Domenico da Piacenza

1) In *PBN 973* and *476*:

19. PREXONERA

Ballo

PBN 972, f. 14v.   Domenico da Piacenza

1) Mensuration sign for *tempus perfectum maioris prolationis* indicated in *PBN 973*.
2) Melody in *PBN 476* a fourth lower.
   From bars 20 to 26 *PBN 476* reads:
3) Mensuration sign for *tempus perfectum maioris prolationis* indicated in this MS.

20. RE DI SPAGNA

Tenore da Bassadanza

RBV, C 203; f. 32r-32v.

Antonio Cornazano

Choreography: Not preserved.

Remarks: This *bassadanza* tenor melody must have enjoyed international popularity for it served as a *bassedanse* titled, CASULLE LA NOVELE (CASTILLE LA NOU-VELLE) found in ToulABD, No. 10. 361 compositions based on this dance tune have been located (GomCMVC, xli-xliii).

The original melody consists of imperfect semibreves except notes 6 and 7 which are *minimae* and the last note a *longa*. My transcription is based on the symbol Ⅽ indicative of *tempus imperfectum maioris prolationis* (6/8).

Editions: BrainTCD, 8-13; BukoPBDR, 195ff; CranMSF, 13 and 72-75, here titled CASTILLE LA NOVELE with a list of other sources where the tune served as a *cantus firmus*; GomCMVC, xli-xliii; HertzSBD, 140; Hughes IM, 151-152; MeyEMBD, 22 and *passim*.

21. ROSTIBOLI GIOIOSO

Ballo

PBN 476, f. 66r.   Giovanni Ambrogio

1. Compare this version with those in Hughes IM, p. 102-106.

2. Superfluous *pausa semibrevis* omitted in transcription.
3. Mensuration sign indicated *proportio dupla*.

22. SOBRIA

Ballo

PBN 972, f. 22r-22v.

Domenico da Piacenza

1) No clef sign in MS.

2) G flat in lieu of E flat in *RBV*.
3) *Tempus perfectum minoris prolationis* in MS.   4) *Semiminima* in *RBV*.

23. SPERO

Ballo

PBN 973, f. 50r.

Guglielmo Ebreo da Pesaro

1) Mensuration sign in *PBN 476*;
   No B flat in *PBN 476*.
2) *Pausa semibrevis* in MS.
3) *Pausa semibrevis* in MS.
4) Mensuration sign in *PBN 476*.
5) *Pausa semibrevis* in MS.

6) *Pausa semibrevis* in MS.
7) The original notation is in dotted
   semibreves: *longae* in *PBN 476*.
   Mensuration sign in error.
8) *Pausa semibrevis* in MS.
9) *Pausa semibrevis* in MS.

24. TESARA

Ballo

PBN 972, f. 23v-24r.   Domenico da Piacenza

25. VERÇEPPE

Ballo

PBN 972, f. 13r.   Domenico da Piacenza

1) *Semibrevis* in MS.   2) *Semibrevis* in MS.   3) Added editor's measure.

26. VOLTATE IN ÇA ROSINA

Ballo

PBN 476, f. 64v.   Giovanni Ambrogio

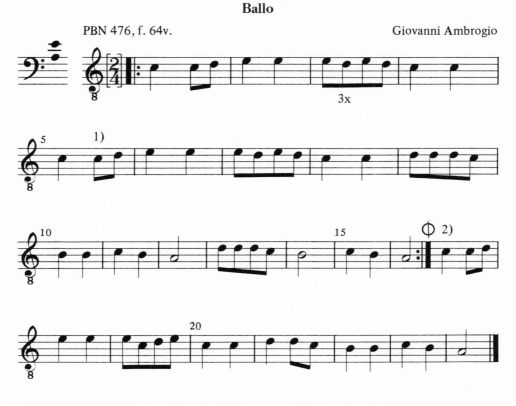

1) *Semibrevis* in MS.
2) The mensuration sign indicates *proportio tripla*.

Information about the Author

Dr. W. Thomas Marrocco is professor emeritus, UCLA. Born in New Jersey, he received his musical education at the Royal Conservatory of Music, Naples, Italy; the Eastman School of Music (B.M. and M.A.); and the University of California (Ph.D.).

A recipient of two Fulbright lectureships and fellowships, three awards from the American Council of Learned Societies, and two grants from the American Philosophical Society, Dr. Marrocco has published in the areas of medieval music and American music. During his tenure at UCLA, he was a member of the Roth String Quartet which concertized here and abroad. Among its recordings are quartets by Ernst Toch, Op. 74; Vernon Duke's *Quartet in C*; and two quintets by Michael Haydn.

Publications include six volumes of Italian secular music for the monumental series, *Polyphonic Music of the Fourteenth Century*, Editions de l'Oiseau-Lyre, Monaco (1967–1977); *Music in America* (with Harold Gleason), New York, Norton, 1964; *Medieval Music* (with Nicholas Sandon), Oxford University Press, London, 1977; numerous articles on Italian and American music in *Acta Musicologica, Journal of the American Musicological Society, Musical Quarterly*, and *Speculum*; and eighty entries in the new *Grove's Dictionary of Music and Musicians*. For his work in the field of Italian music and the propagation of Italian language and culture he was awarded the Order of Merit by the Italian government.

Dance research includes a study (with Dr. Emma Lewis Thomas) of fourteenth century Italian dances as described by Giovanni Boccaccio in his *Decameron* (JDR, X, 1971, 19) and "The Derivation of another Bassadanza," demonstrating the derivation of the bassadanza melody, Collinetto, from the French chanson, *Biance flour* (*Acta Musicologica*, LI, 1979, 137). A work (with Marie Laure Milbank) on an English translation of Antonio Arena's *Ad suos compagnones* (Lyons, 1529) is in preparation.

Information About CORD

Cord Publications

Dance Research Annual* — a series consisting either of manuscripts and proceedings directly related to CORD-sponsored conferences or to manuscripts submitted for publication in non-conference years.

I   RESEARCH IN DANCE: PROBLEMS AND POSSIBILITIES (proceedings of the 1967 Preliminary Conference on Research in Dance held at Greyston House, Riverdale, N.Y.), Richard Bull, ed., 1968.

II   WORKSHOPS ON DANCE THERAPY: Its Research Potentials (therapy approaches and evaluations of them presented at the 1968 workshop sponsored jointly by the American Dance Therapy Association, the Postgraduate Center for Mental Health and CORD), 1970.

III   DANCE HISTORY RESEARCH: Perspectives from Related Arts and Disciplines (proceedings of the 1969 CORD Conference held at Airlie House, Warrenton, Virginia), Joann Kealiinohomoku, ed., 1970.

IV   INSTITUTE OF COURT DANCES OF THE RENAISSANCE AND BAROQUE PERIODS (review of the Dance Notation Bureau-sponsored institutes held at Lake Fairlee Camp, Ely, Vermont, in August-September, 1970, and Mt. Holyoke College in August-September, 1971), Juana de Laban, ed., 1972.

V   DANCE RESEARCH MONOGRAPH ONE (a collection of dance articles contributed by CORD members), Patricia A. Rowe and Ernestine Stodelle, eds., 1973.

---

*Unit Price Annuals I-V, $7.50; Annuals VI-XIII, $10.00

VI NEW DIMENSIONS IN DANCE RESEARCH: ANTHROPOL-OGY AND DANCE — THE AMERICAN INDIAN (proceedings of the Third CORD Conference, held in March-April, 1972 at the University of Arizona, Tucson and the Tucson Yaqui Villages), Tamara Comstock, ed., 1974.

VII RESEARCH MONOGRAPH TWO — REFLECTIONS AND PERSPECTIVES ON TWO ANTHROPOLOGICAL STUDIES OF DANCE: A Comparative Study of Dance as a Constellation of Motor Behaviors Among African and United States Negroes, by J.W. Kealiinohomoku; and The Dance of the Taos Pueblo, by D.N. Brown, Adrienne L. Kaeppler, ed., 1974.

VIII ASIAN AND PACIFIC DANCE: Selected papers from the 1974 San Francisco CORD-SEM Conference, Adrienne L. Kaeppler, Judy Van Zile, Carl Wolz, eds., 1977.

IX ESSAYS IN DANCE RESEARCH (selected papers from the 1976 Philadelphia CORD/ADG Conference), Dianne L. Woodruff, ed., 1978.

X DANCE RESEARCH COLLAGE: A Variety of Subjects Embracing the Abstract and the Practical, Patricia A. Rowe and Ernestine Stodelle, eds., 1979.

XI PSYCHOLOGICAL PERSPECTIVES ON DANCE (selected papers from the San Francisco CORD/SEM Conference-based series II), Ruth E. Priddle, ed., 1978.

XII KATHERINE DUNHAM: REFLECTIONS ON THE SOCIAL AND POLITICAL CONTEXTS OF AFRO-AMERICAN DANCE by Joyce Aschenbrenner, with NOTATIONS OF THE DUNHAM METHOD AND TECHNIQUE by Lavinia Williams, Patricia A. Rowe, ed., 1981.

Dance Research Journal — a semi-annual (fall/spring) periodical that includes articles, reviews, research materials and announcements (formerly CORD News).

CORD News — Vol. I (1969)–Vol. VI (1974). Back issues available at $4.00 per single issue.

Dance Research Journal — Vol. VII–Vol. XII/1. Back issues available at $5.00 per single issue.

Dance Research Specials — TWO ESSAYS ON STEPANOV DANCE NOTA-TION: I. Table of Signs for the Notation of the Movements of the Human Body According to the System of V.I. Stepanov; II. Choreography..., by Alexander Gorsky, trans. by Roland John Wiley, 1978.

Publications In Progress

XIV   TRADITIONAL DANCE IN THE 20TH CENTURY, Emphasis on Asian and Pacific Dance, I, (proceedings and selected papers from the 1978 CORD/ADG Hawaii Conference), Betty True Jones, ed.-in-chf., (free to 1981–82 members).

XV   TRADITIONAL DANCE IN THE 20TH CENTURY, Emphasis on Asian and Pacific Dance, II, (proceedings and selected papers from the 1978 CORD/ADG Hawaii Conference), Betty True Jones, ed.-in-chf., (free to 1982–83 members).

To order CORD Publications: Specify volume and number for *Dance Research Journal*, the title or number for *Dance Research Annual* or *Special Publication*, number of copies desired, price per unit and total. Multiple copies of publications are available at bulk rates on pre-paid orders: 20 per cent discount for 10 or more copies. Supply a clearly typed or printed shipping address. Send a check or money order in U.S. funds, payable to Cord Inc.

Manuscripts

Submit manuscripts in duplicate *to the attention* of: Chairman, Editorial Board *or* Editor, *DRA or* Editor, *DRJ.* Include a self-addressed envelope stamped for return of one copy to the sender. Manuscripts should conform to style specifications set in A MANUAL OF STYLE, 12th Ed., (University of Chicago Press, 1969). Notes must appear on a separate page at the end of the document. Only materials conforming to these regulations will be reviewed.

Membership Information

The Congress on Research in Dance is an international, interdisciplinary, open membership organization. Its purposes are 1) to encourage research in all aspects of dance, including its related fields; 2) to foster the exchange of ideas, resources and methodology through publications, international and regional conferences and workshops; 3) to promote the accessibility of research materials.

CORD annual membership is available in the following categories:

> General Membership: Regular ($30); Institutional ($50); Student ($20); Senior Citizen ($10)

> Donor Membership: Patron ($1,000); Sponsor ($500); Donor ($100); Friend ($60); Sustaining ($50).

Members of CORD have voting privileges, reduced rates at conferences, special discounts on CORD publications, and receive two journals and one annual publication each membership year (September 1–August 31).

1980–1981 Board of Directors

1978–1981	1979–1982	1980–1983
Betty True Jones	Selma Jeanne Cohen	Nancy M. Bodenstein
Genevieve Oswald	Judith Brin Ingber	Margaret T. Drewel (to 1981)
Jeanette Roosevelt	Miriam Morrison	Angelika Gerbes
Anthony Shay	Jerry Duke	Nancy Lee Ruyter
Roland John Wiley	Lynne Weber	Jill D. Sweet

Past Chairmen: Elizabeth Burtner, Patricia A. Rowe

1980–1981 Executive Committee

Joyce R. Malm, *Chairman*

Past-Chairman, Ingrid Brainard   *Recording Secretary,* Mary Jane Warner
Treasurer, Elsie I. Dunin   *Corresponding Secretary,* Ruth K. Abrahams

1980–1981 Editorial Board

Patricia A. Rowe, *Chairman*

Ruth K. Abrahams	Adrienne L. Kaeppler
Selma Jeanne Cohen	James M. Murphy

CRA and **CRJ**

are two benefits of membership in

Why wait?

Join now!

Congress on Research in Dance
NYU Dance and Dance Education Dept.
35 West Fourth Street, Room 675
New York, NY 10003

NEW PUBLICATION

TUTELO RITUALS ON SIX NATIONS RESERVE, ONTARIO

by
Gertrude Prokosch Kurath

This prolific author reports on her thirty-year interest in the Tutelo Indian tribe from the time of their known seventeenth century origins in what is now Virginia. Located with the Iroquois on Six Nations Reserve, Ontario, the Tutelo's influence on rituals of the Iroquois is evidenced today in three great ceremonies (*Four Nights Harvest Dance*, *Fourth Night Spirit Release Singing*, *Spirit Adoption Ceremony*) described in detail, liberally illustrated and stylistically evaluated in this work.

ORDER FROM:

CORD, Inc. — N.Y. Office
@ $8.00
(includes postage & handling)

A 1981 publication by SEM with printing co-sponsorship by CORD.

NOTES

NOTES